MW00769640

PRAISE FOR 50 STATES OF MIND

"If you are sadly convinced that our country is hopelessly divided along political and cultural lines, then I strongly urge you to read the book that is guaranteed to give you hope."

— CONGRESSWOMAN JAN SCHAKOWSKY

"Ryan Bernsten gives us a window into our vast complexity, how we are different and yet alike. At a time of depressing headlines and news stories, *50 States of Mind* provides a welcome antidote and restores hope that our country will be all right in the end."

— GOVERNOR CHRISTINE TODD WHITMAN

"A chatty and engaging road trip into the many hearts of America."

— *KIRKUS REVIEWS*

"An endless adventure through the 50 states... it will go a long way to addressing many issues that we are currently facing. This book is a must-read."

— FRANK MUTUMA, *READERS' FAVORITE*
(STARRED REVIEW)

"Any politician, whether aspiring or actively in office, would do well to heed the words of *50 States of Mind*... the book's much-needed prescription for angst and depression provides hope and a sense of purpose to modern America's struggles which is largely missing from newspaper headlines, but encouragingly present in this book. It considers the influences that polarize America, the nation's hopeful possibilities, and the pulse of a people living, breathing, and interacting to create a new American story."

— *THE MIDWEST BOOK REVIEW*

"Clear-eyed, searching, and hopeful, *50 States of Mind* reminds us that democracy is not a perpetual motion machine. Without the kind of open-hearted curiosity that fueled Ryan Bernsten's powerfully moving cross-country journey, this all falls apart. With it, America has a future."

— SAMANTHA ALLEN, AUTHOR OF *REAL QUEER AMERICA: LGBT STORIES FROM RED STATES*

"Soulful, refreshing, and surprisingly funny, *50 States of Mind* cuts through the divisive noise of the political moment. By approaching those he meets with humility and a commitment to listening, Ryan creates a portrait of the country which shows that, at the end of the day, most Americans have the same goals: strong communities and hope for the future."

— JASON KANDER, FORMER MISSOURI SECRETARY OF STATE, U.S. SENATE CANDIDATE, HOST OF MAJORITY 54 PODCAST

50 STATES OF MIND

A Journey to Rediscover American Democracy

RYAN BERNSTEN

Published by Bite-Sized Books Ltd 2023

© Ryan Bernsten 2023

Bite-Sized Books Limited

16 High Holborn, London, WC1V 6BX, England

Registered in the UK. Company Registration No: 9395379

Bite-Sized Books Hardcover ISBN: 978-1-7393107-2-1

Bite-Sized Books Paperback ISBN: 978-1-7393107-4-5

eBook ISBN: 978-1-7393107-0-7

Audiobook ISBN: 978-1-7393107-5-2

The moral right of Ryan Bernsten to be identified as the author of this work has been asserted by him in accordance with the Copyright, Designs and Patents Act 1988.

All rights reserved. No part of this publication may be reproduced without the prior permission of the publishers.

Cover by Dean Stockton. Photos by Michael Demarco, Jurij Vlasov.

To the Americans who invited me in and told me their stories — thank you.

PREFACE

The pulse of America is elusive. There is no steady beat; there is only the erratic rhythm of a people with very little shared history constantly rediscovering how to live together. Despite this, I—a staffer from a failed 2016 presidential campaign—read *Democracy in America* in graduate school, found inspiration in Alexis de Tocqueville's travels, and decided to follow in his footsteps nearly 180 years after his book's publication. I hit the road to talk to Americans of all stripes; with a grant from my graduate program at the University of Oxford, I drove 23,257 miles to visit over 150 cities, towns, and villages in all 50 states. I wanted to find answers to the defining questions of the era. Does American democracy still work? Can we still coexist peacefully? Amidst the horror of national headlines, I wasn't expecting to find something optimistic on the ground. I wasn't expecting to have to question my own place in our democracy. And I certainly wasn't expecting to find myself living somewhere new at the end of it.

After the 2016 election, I wanted to understand the complicated country I lived in and where I fit into it. The question of what it means to be an American has always been difficult in a country so full of various cultures and viewpoints, let alone during such a polarized time. To accurately portray America's staggering diversity, I pushed myself to meet people from all walks of life. My mission was to listen not teach, to learn not lecture, and my only methodology was the desire to find someone unlike anyone else I had met before. I stayed in the homes of people across the country who opened their doors to me. In turn, I responded with an open mind and a generous ear. If I hadn't, this trip would not have been possible. This mindset also gave me space to learn what I didn't know about the diverse perspectives across our country. I found a surprising amount of common ground, and it became my belief that building bridges—even with those with whom we initially seem to disagree—could be our last line of defense against a quickly radicalizing society; the breakdown of candid dialogue benefited only the powers profiting off our division and outrage, lest we realize how much we actually agree on. The late great Secretary of State Madeleine Albright crystalized the dangers of our political environment in her book *Fascism: A Warning*: "At many levels, contempt has become a defining characteristic of American politics. It makes us unwilling to listen to what others say—unwilling, in some cases, even to allow them to speak. This stops the learning process cold and creates a ready-made audience for demagogues who know how to bring diverse groups of the aggrieved together in righteous opposition to everyone else." With her words in mind, I consciously tried to rid myself of any vestige of self-righteousness or contempt as I allowed my preconceived notions to be challenged by my fellow Americans. I hope you'll have your preconceived notions challenged too. Only then can we see what is within the bounds of normalcy and what is dangerous extremism, and be able to recognize the latter when we see it.

Ultimately, American democracy is made up of unique states of mind and stories that inform every citizen's worldview. By deciding to start with the people, I was reminded that America is a community existing together in a shared moment with far more in common than that which divides us. We have so much to learn from each other. I hope this book can take you on a journey to challenge your understanding of the United States through the small interactions I had with people all across the nation. By offering a sampling of the staggering diversity in America, I hope you experience the wonders, contradictions, oddities, and thrills of 50 very different states of mind.

THE HOMETOWN

"I SEE YOUR POINT," I said to my parents, grimly sitting across from me in my childhood home just outside of Rockford, Illinois.

I was an idealist, a big plan-maker, but the gravity of what I had set out to do was crashing down on me. A broke grad student with a list of careers that spanned from birthday party clown to English teacher to actor to sushi waiter to presidential campaign staffer, I had never stuck around long in one place. When I returned home to explain what I had just signed up for, I could see in my parents' faces that I had confirmed their worst fears that I was permanently transient.

Dad rubbed his eyes. "Explain it to me again."

"I'm going to drive to all 50 states."

"To do… what?" Mom asked.

"To figure out what went wrong with democracy in America."

The fire crackled dramatically. Of course you are.

My life was thrown off track the year before. I had spent my years out of college bouncing around between the largest cities—Chicago, New York, Los Angeles—before I returned to my small-town roots with a job on a 2016 presidential campaign. Originally from Rockford, a Rust Belt town in the Midwest, I felt at home in rural and overlooked parts of the country. I loved organizing teams of volunteers, from dairy farmers in Iowa to Haitian immigrants in Florida. On the campaign, I had spoken to disaffected Democrats but no Republicans; the campaign's strategy was to turn out our base, not reach out to those with whom we disagreed. As someone from a family where everyone identified as commonsense Democrats, I felt there was a large swath of the country whose perspectives I had never encountered.

After an election that didn't go as planned, I was left questioning my vision of America and my role in it. Instead of heading to Washington in victory for a job in the administration, I found myself driving back to my parents' house in Rockford. I do my best thinking in the car, and the questions vexing me on that 20-hour drive home from Florida continued to dog me on many drives to come. What did we miss? What did I have to learn? And why couldn't I seem to stay in one place?

After three months of stewing, I wrote a grad school application essay about my existential crisis and was accepted to graduate school at the University of Oxford. Once again, this meant moving, the only state of being that I seemed to exist in. I left the United States for Oxford's libraries, met a cohort of friends from all over the globe, and annoyed them all through my endless late-night pub assessments of 2016. But how could I not? Reading the American news filled me with dismay, but I tried every angle for a silver lining. At my core, I was an optimist. How could I turn America's trajectory (and my own life) being blown off course into a positive? I felt if I could solve the riddle of what was happening to my country, I could solve the question of where I fit into it.

Unfortunately, my obsession with what was happening back home was interfering with the very real academic need to come up with an idea for my thesis to justify my time at Oxford. I was chronically single, had no permanent address, and had no clue what I wanted to do with my life. What could I possibly write about for my 25,000-word thesis?

The answer revealed itself thanks to a happy accident in the Bodleian Library's shelving system. On the book reservation shelf sat my copy of *Bowling Alone,* next to a book I had only heard of in my history classes: Alexis de Tocqueville's *Democracy in America.* Delaying my study day, I picked up the book and started to read about a Frenchman's journey to get the pulse of American democracy in 1831. I was taken by how familiar his observations seemed as he dissected a sensationalist press and a populace that decried their President as a "heartless despot, solely occupied with the preservation of his own authority" who "governs by means of corruption," referring to the divisive, populist President Andrew Jackson. I read on, taken by the French writer's eloquence, objectivity, and nuance. Daunted by the weight of the task he had undertaken, I was shocked to find that when de Tocqueville went on his journey through America, he was only 26—the exact same age that I was, reading in the library. Was this French dude from the 1800s the answer to my quest for purpose?

I thought of the state of democracy in America. It was not going well. My friends on the campaign had been the types who constantly poked fun at the perceptions of fellow Democrats as snowflakes and woke ideologues, and I always felt I was able to laugh at myself and look at situations with humor and objectivity. These days, being self-critical seemed anathema to the state of America. Those in power and the media profited off division and the American population constantly took the bait. I was tired of daily social media feuds. I was tired of hypocritical hysterics on the right. I was tired of having to defend the Midwest from the slander of liberal city-dwellers. The disappearance of empathy had become an epidemic, and there was a refusal to put the finger on the real pulse of America: its citizens. As the dying light illuminated Oxford's creamy stone buildings and ancient clock towers with a rosy glow, I realized people needed to talk face to face. I passed students conversing in Latin and wearing billowing black sub fusc robes on their way to formal dinners in medieval dining halls, and I figured maybe I needed a dose of reality.

I went to my graduate department and proposed an idea for my thesis: I would follow de Tocqueville's model of traveling across America by visiting all 50 states to meet people on the ground. Expecting my advisors to help me come up with something more manageable, I was surprised when they rubber-stamped the gambit instead. I thought they knew me better; this was certainly far too broad and far too ambitious for someone with my American over-confidence, but instead they gave me a green light to take advantage of the five-month period for field research built into the curriculum to travel the United States. That settled that.

I spent the next few weeks trying to get myself into the mindset of permanent transience. I pictured what my days would look like; it was a mixture of the listening tours I had seen presidential candidates make in Iowa and *Diners, Drive-Ins and Dives* on the Food Network; if I wasn't confident in my ability to find answers about democracy, I was at least sure of my ability to eat my way through America's diverse and flourishing food landscape. In October of 2018, I left the town of dreaming spires and returned to my hometown of Rockford, Illinois, stunned by the enormity of the task that I had set myself up for.

The excitement of the mission was fading now, looking at my parents' worried faces. I wondered how de Tocqueville's parents felt when he left for America.

Dad sighed. "Where will you stay?"

A few days prior, I had posted a Facebook status about my trip and received over a hundred responses offering couches to crash on across America, ranging from people I had met on the campaign to friends of friends from college. According to my spreadsheet, I allegedly had places to stay in 40 states. I eagerly explained the generosity I had encountered on the internet, watching their expressions turn from pity to alarm.

4

"So you're staying with… strangers?"

I paused. "A few."

This was the final straw. I had a traumatizing couch-surfing experience three years prior involving a nudist in the most dangerous area of San Francisco, a story that trickled its way to my parents through my grandma and caused them to doubt my judgment forever. Mom said she needed to go to bed. I watched her leave, rubbing her temples. Dad sat down next to the fire, looking serious.

"You're 26 now—"

The same age as de Tocqueville was!

"You've been jumping around from place to place, job to job, now leaving Oxford —"

I had to do research!

"—it can't hurt to think about—"

I'm going to save democracy, Dad!

"—law school."

I knew that my father was looking ahead to my thirties and visualizing where my current trajectory would take me: living in a van down by the river.

"I'll think about it," I said, but diving into the heart of our ailing democracy felt more urgent than studying for a law school exam. The truth was, I thrived on taking leaps of faith like this; I had learned to trust that a net would inevitably appear. Some combo of charm and privilege and audacity and enterprise had kept me optimistic that risk was the spice of life, and now I was gambling on the hospitality of the American people. Maybe jumping into the unknown without a safety net was exactly the adventure I craved. The turmoil of politics had trickled into the American psyche, and I needed to find some faith in my fellow Americans in an increasingly stormy world.

My mom's voice rang from her bedroom. "You don't even have a car!"

The next day, I emptied my savings to buy a car. In the lot of my local dealership, I spotted a midnight black Prius sporting a black and white interior, like an orca whale. It was love at first sight. From the moment I got behind the wheel, I knew she was my travel companion. Steinbeck had Charley. I had Belinda.

I spent the next few days packing for the trip. It had been such a long time since I had been home, and I felt a strong sense of nostalgia going through my childhood room. The possessions I had accumulated, souvenirs from trips I had taken, letters and notes from friends and exes, posters from campaigns I had worked on. I was only 26, but it seemed I had been traveling everywhere to find myself. There was a sense that I was always running towards something—or away from it.

Before I left Rockford, it felt important to drive around the city to root myself. I drove through my hometown, introducing Belinda to the city where I came of age. As we drove past Blain's Farm and Fleet and the condemned Clock Tower Resort, I realized that Rockford had been the last place I had called home.

Rockford was "Screw City," a manufacturing giant and America's number one exporter of screws. Rumor has it that we were third on Hitler's bomb list—a pretty badass thing for the third-largest city in Illinois (population 146,526). In the 1970s, however, Rockford joined other screwed cities where manufacturing jobs were disappearing. In the wake of the Great Recession, Rockford's unemployment rate hit 12.5% in 2008, spiked at 17.3% in 2010 when I was a senior in high school, and finally returned to high single digits in 2014, according to the Bureau of Labor Statistics. We're also the town that became meme famous after voting "Taco Bell" its number one Mexican restaurant. Because of crime and closed factories, Rockford gained further notoriety after Forbes ranked it the "Third Most Miserable City in America" around the time I left for college. Rockford took the ranking as a challenge and began actively revitalizing both the town and its morale. Rockfordians are survivors: scrappy, wry, generous, and kind.

Where I grew up was foundational to my understanding of my country; my worldview was a product of where I came from. We drove through Rockford's East Side down towards the river. The East Side is a largely suburban area, full of former cornfields turned into strip malls that lured in new restaurants to open, die, and be replaced by tanning salons when I was growing up. We drove alongside the Rock River, the muddy divide which separates Rockford into two sides of town and states of mind and eventually crossed a bridge to the West Side. We approached the skeleton of my former childhood haven, New American Theatre, which now sat empty. I still remember everything about the downtown theater, from the coffee-scented rehearsal studio to the rusty metal stairwell that boomed so loudly that you had to tiptoe to not be heard onstage. I spent my formative years doing theatre at this playhouse. New American Theatre progressively transformed into a second home. The theater glowed with a sense of professionalism, but even more astounding was the strong community bond that formed within the company. Friendships that solidified backstage were so adhesive that many still played central roles in my life. I grew up at NAT; many can attest to my transformation from a boisterous youngster to a young man within the building that now sat empty. I lost that home in 2008; NAT closed during the recession. Everywhere I go, whether Iowa or London, I think about the boy crying on the phone after getting the call that the doors to New American Theatre would never open again, and remind myself the debt I owe to that kid, to Rockford, to other places labeled "miserable." I knew the people I would meet across the country were also a product of their upbringings and communities. I pledged to remember this and to approach them with an open mind.

After five years in the major cities, traveling on campaigns, and crossing the ocean for grad school, I hoped this 50-state journey would close the chapter on that period of transience. As I drove home for one final night, I hoped I was on the precipice of something more than a series of toll roads, gas stations, and highway exits. It was October in the Midwest, my favorite time of year. As Belinda and I drew closer to home, I passed farms surrounded by golden woods and found myself hoping I would someday find my own place in America.

THE FIRST STATE

MY JOURNEY BEGAN—AS most do—with a late start. An hour behind schedule, I climbed into my Toyota Prius at 8:30 a.m. on October 17th, 2018. I grabbed the steering wheel, turned on Simon & Garfunkel's *America*, and set off on my journey, too rushed to fully savor the beginning of the five-month trip.

I merged onto the highway and drove towards the Buckeye State. Ohio was the heart of the country: a swing state that had—at the time, at least—voted for the winner of every single presidential election since 1960, electing diametrically opposed personalities such as Obama and Trump, Carter and Reagan. If I wanted to get America's pulse, Ohio was the place to start. As I drove across the state line under a suspension bridge, I felt the indescribable change in atmosphere that comes from entering a new state. Suddenly, there were trees flanking the side of the highway, seemingly planted to welcome new visitors to the state ahead of a sign that read "Ohio: Find It Here." I hoped this was a good omen that I would find answers in Ohio.

I was on my way to Gambier (population 2,391). Even though it was home to Kenyon College, a remote liberal arts school, Knox

County was a deeply conservative, rural area. I exited the highway onto a country road that ran through rolling farms and one-stop-light towns. With farmland on my right and a wooded hill on my left, I turned towards the hill and ascended into the tiny village of Gambier. I drove alongside the Kenyon College campus and parked outside of city hall, a one-story concrete building connected to the town library. I was meeting the mayor of Gambier, J. Kachen Kimmel. Upon entering the office, I found a petite, scrappy blonde woman sitting behind the desk. She grasped my hand.

"Nice to meet you, mayor," I said, starting to sit.

She stopped me and pointed to a red Tupperware full of chocolate chip cookies on her desk. "Grab a cookie. You're not spending your time in Gambier stuck in an office." She thrust a cookie into my hand and yanked me outside to the town Jeep.

"Well? Get in!"

Kachen put the Jeep in reverse, looking over her shoulder as she backed out of the lot.

We were speeding along a gravel road towards town when Kachen turned to me and said, "I think I understand your project."

"What do you mean?"

"You know, big city progressive moves to get to know rural America," she said, jerking the Jeep's stick shift. Kachen drove through the campus full of storm-gray gothic buildings and told me how, after years of practicing law in the Chicago suburbs, she and her husband had an existential crisis. They were making a good living, but they weren't seeing their son enough, spending the bulk of their time commuting and working downtown. On a whim, her husband applied for a job at Kenyon College, his alma mater, and got an offer. The family decided to take a leap of faith: he took the job, they bought an old Victorian house in Gambier, and traded a life in Chicago for one in the middle of Ohio. In rural America for the first time in her adult life, Kachen tried her hand in the Kenyon admissions department before getting into local politics and was eventually elected mayor of a town where, in her office, she's the only Democrat.

She stopped the Jeep, allowing scarf-wrapped students to cross the street into town, and turned to me. "So what made you start here?"

I explained that as a high schooler, Kenyon had been a top choice college. I loved the idea of a remote, gothic campus full of poet-scholars. While I had opted to go to Northwestern, I had returned to the campus twice—once with a friend from Rockford, another time for a playwriting conference—and it seemed only natural to start the journey in a place that both felt like home yet still exotic.

I asked Kachen if she minded me recording our conversation. She eagerly shook her head; I pulled out my tiny hand recorder and put it in the Jeep's cup holder.

"Progressives need to get brave," said Kachen, pounding her fist on the steering wheel. "Maybe it would be easier to clump up in the big cities, but I don't think that helps us on the long road to saving our democracy."

I took in the surroundings, gazing down into the valley where the Kokosing River was flowing under reddening trees. During my visits, I had always been enchanted by the mist shrouding the hills in the morning, the potency of the storms in the afternoon, the fireflies over the river at night.

"Besides," Kachen said, reading my mind, "why should conservatives get the most beautiful parts of the country to themselves?"

She turned onto the main street to give me a tour of downtown Gambier. We passed the coffee shop, post office, inn, and deli, as Kachen occasionally stopped to wave at dog-walkers or rolled down her window to happily chide professors with outstanding parking tickets. We drove towards the countryside, and I asked her what it was like to be a progressive in a county where voters had such different points of view.

"I mean, my staff are all conservative," she said. "Those cookies you ate? Suzie made them. She loves Trump." Kachen explained that she felt national politics was often more of a distraction from getting done what needed to get done in her community. Kachen boiled it down to civility and figuring out how to have a practical conversation. "Out in the county, farmers are installing solar panels. Don't talk to them about alternative energy. Talk to them about this big expanse on the roof of their dairy barn that holds all these solar panels, and they never have to buy electricity to milk their cows again."

She drove past a waste-water treatment plant, and suddenly we were cruising through farmland. "Climate change, to me, is a perfect example of how in real life you find a way to talk to people about how the changing weather is affecting them," she said, pointing to the rolling farms. "If you talk to farmers about the weather, they know it's not the same. And if you ask them, you can engage in that conversation as long as you don't say 'climate change.' I will argue with you on a different day about *why* it's happening, but we can all agree... we've gotten a lot more rain here than we've ever had before."

Growing up, I had watched many adults undertake death-defying logical gymnastics rather than admit that they could be wrong. Still, I had learned that condescendingly forcing someone to admit a mistaken view—whether parents or friends or a partner—was a surefire way of rupturing the relationship. It seemed Kachen had utilized the same tact.

In town, we parked and visited the college bookstore. I walked through the rows of bestsellers, thinking of how perfect Kachen's story was: someone who was actually walking the walk and living among people with different perspectives. I bought her a latte at Wiggins Street Coffee. On the way back to her office, she stopped to chat with a parent and prospective student reading a map. As she shook their hands, I tried picturing her as an overworked lawyer in an office. This Ohio version of Kachen clutching a latte and greeting passersby seemed relaxed, upbeat. Happy.

I imagined myself in Gambier, teaching at the college in the winter and running by the river with a dog in the summer… it seemed ideal, really…

I caught myself. This was my first of hundreds of stops. If I allowed myself to spin a future in every place I visited, I risked getting distracted, or worse, falling in love. I said goodbye to Kachen and got into Belinda before she could show me anything else that seemed picturesque or ideal.

I started driving south toward Columbus, a route that took Belinda off the backroads and merged her back onto the highway. A billboard next to the road warned "HELL IS REAL."

I was heading to Worthington (population 13,575), a suburb of Columbus, to have dinner with Andrew Lippa. Andrew is the president of the Dramatist's Guild and the writer/composer of Broadway musicals such as *The Wild Party*, *The Addams Family*, and *Big Fish*. He was a recent transplant to Ohio after living in New York for decades, and I was curious to find out more about his transition back to the heartland. I arrived at the Whitney House restaurant to find Andrew and his fiancé Tom waiting for me. Tom was a music teacher and a professional musician who plays in orchestras across the country when he's not teaching the youth of America. I told him about how ideal life in Gambier seemed.

"*Exactly*," Tom said, nodding his head. "Honestly, I love traveling, but it's just so nice to be part of a community. After summers playing in orchestras, my job is a respite. It's like, after the craziness of New York, all I have to do is teach kids music for eight hours a day? Great!"

"I'll always love New York, but I really can write from anywhere," Andrew told me. "And I actually feel like after 2016, I can make an impact here. I've gotten involved with the Human Rights Campaign in Ohio. If I was doing that in New York, big deal. Here, it matters. I come in and I say, 'I know people on Broadway. Can we do a concert here, what can we do?'"

This trip was about democracy, not presidential elections, but I was aware of the impact each voter could have in a swing state. The question of the Electoral College had been vexing me for years. In one third of the presidential elections during my lifetime, candidates who had lost the popular vote but won the Electoral College had gone on to remake the country with a mandate that they did not earn. Had the Electoral College failed us or had we failed the Electoral College? If three million people had chosen to live in places like Wisconsin, Pennsylvania, or Ohio, we would be living in a very different political reality. *The Atlantic* writer Derek Thompson crystalizes the situation in a series of articles about the slow exodus of blue voters to the largest urban areas, declaring that if liberals continue to pack themselves on the urban coasts, "the U.S. may be doomed to replay the 2016 election for several more cycles. Coastal liberals will remain justifiably furious that their votes are systematically discounted, while rural conservatives will remain justifiably indignant that the heart of American business and media has flocked to cities that regard the countryside as a xenophobic backwater." Many people saw the Electoral College as archaic; to me, its power to override the will of the majority was a warning that too many like-minded people had clustered in the largest cites, abandoning the vital communities across America. Kachen and Andrew, both transplants from the top three metro areas, made the case that living in the heartland was also in their best economic and social interest.

In an era where cities like Austin, Nashville, and Denver have infrastructure groaning under an avalanche of new residents, Cleveland (population 385,525) has seen a loss of manufacturing jobs, cutting its population in half since its peak of 914,000 in the

1960s. Cleveland is also a city that saw the rise of African American political power with figures like Carl Stokes—the first black mayor of Cleveland—and his brother Louis Stokes, a 15-term congressman. When Barack Obama was mulling a run for president in 2006, he came to Cleveland looking for answers. He must have found some: he won Ohio twice.

I arrived at a taco restaurant called Bakersfield to meet Austin, a local news anchor and a friend from high school. Austin was there with his co-worker Ram, a Cleveland native of Jamaican heritage who relentlessly gave Austin shit about his meticulously coiffed hair. I instantly liked him. Austin told me that Ram had started an organization called InnerCity Baseball, which focused on using the sport to get college paid for, rather than getting into the major leagues.

"We also take girls as well," Ram said, ordering a beer. "We just want people playing the game."

When Austin told Ram about my desire to see "Real Cleveland," Ram thought of the perfect place: a historically Black bar called Skeets VSP. "You've got to see highbrow, middlebrow, and lowbrow," Ram told me. "Cleveland does all three." I loved the idea of replicating Ram's "brow" method as I traveled around the country. Ram told Austin to take me around the West Side to see "highbrow," and he would meet us later on to provide the rest.

We started with the West Side Market, a cavernous hall reminiscent of a train station, with rows and rows of vendors selling everything from fudge to soul food. Austin and I were given free beers by the owner of the West Side Market Cafe because they recognized him from the news, and just because it was my first time in Cleveland. After sampling some fudge, we drove down to Public Square at the foot of the 52-story Terminal Tower, once the tallest building in the world besides the Empire State Building. We drove through the downtown, past historic brick buildings with new restaurants and the Rock & Roll Hall of Fame on the lakefront. We turned a corner, and I was shocked to find a giant chandelier hanging above an intersection. I learned that this was Cleveland's Playhouse Square—the largest concentration of theaters in any American city outside of New York. I hadn't expected Cleveland to be a proper metropolis or to have outdoor lighting fixtures like the set of *Phantom of the Opera*.

As we snapped photos in front of the giant CLEVELAND sign that was picture-perfectly positioned in front of the skyline, I turned to Austin.

"I don't understand why everyone instantly flocks to Chicago and New York," I said. Cleveland, which I had always heard referred to as "The Mistake on the Lake" seemed anything but. "A city like this is the perfect size to make an impact."

"Or at least to get recognized enough to get a free beer every once in a while." Austin grinned as he picked up a phone call. It was Ram.

"Are you boys ready for a little East Side experience?"

East Cleveland reminded me a lot of West Rockford in the 2000s. There was a general sense that a blind eye from the city government had allowed the infrastructure to fall into a state of disrepair, and a sense that neighborhoods like the Union Miles Park area were not frequented by those in power. According to a map from Trulia, we were driving towards one of the highest-crime intersections in Cleveland. As I imagined de Tocqueville rolling up to Skeets in a French waistcoat and top hat, I was reminded of the sobering fact that inequalities in our cities were the products of injustices that de Tocqueville failed to mention while lauding equality in 1831 America. East Cleveland was a reminder that racial inequality does not disappear on its own throughout the generations. Austin and I parked at the corner of 93rd and Gibson and walked up the cracked sidewalk to the door of Skeets VSP Lounge.

"Should we wait for Ram?" Austin asked. He glanced nervously at the intersection we had just read about.

"Nah, let's go in."

It was an after-work crowd inside Skeets. The appearance of two white guys in the all-Black bar was not as nonchalant as I had hoped. We sat at the bar, waiting for Ram. I smiled back as people gave us curious nods or just stared. *I'm glad I didn't make this a documentary,* I thought, picturing rolling into the bar with a camera crew. Recording already gave a slight edge to conversations, and I couldn't imagine shoving a camera in someone's face and expecting them to be totally candid. There was no way to communicate that I was there to learn, not pull a stunt, and the question of "what the hell are you doing here?" was clear in every suspicious glance thrown our way.

Finally, Ram arrived. We ordered drinks and the three of us sat at the bar talking amongst ourselves, struggling to break our invisible barrier. This is why people don't leave their comfort zones, I realized: it can be awkward. Austin and Ram were shifting uncomfortably, taking cues off my unease.

I wasn't going to set the tone for the next 49 states by being timid; I took a deep breath and turned to the man sitting next to me. "How's your day going?"

He smiled and shook his head, amused that I had finally started to talk. "What are you doing here, man?"

I looked around at the bar, where everyone was watching me out of the corner of their eye. "I'm traveling to all 50 states to talk to people about their communities."

"All 50 states!"

"Yeah, and Ohio is my first stop."

The man gave me a high five. "And you chose the best place in Ohio."

Suddenly, the people who had been watching us from around the bar started gathering.

"What brings you here?"

"He wants to hear about the neighborhood!"

"You want to hear about the neighborhood? We'll tell you about the neighborhood!"

I discovered that I was surrounded by sheet metal workers, mechanics, and veterans who had lived in the area for decades, some for their whole lives. Everyone I talked to seemed excited that I had chosen Skeets as a place to showcase the Ohio state of mind.

Rio, a straight-shooter in a hoodie, stood and listened as the older folks at the bar told me how they had grown up with Hollywood actor Bill Cobbs and how his success made him an icon of hometown pride. After listening to this, Rio approached, told me that he admired my hustle, and asked if I wanted to step outside for a recorded interview that "didn't sugarcoat things."

Outside, the streets were dark. Rio told me he didn't want me getting a falsely rosy impression of the neighborhood and asked candidly what I was looking for at Skeets.

"The real Cleveland," I said, holding up my recorder.

He nodded and pointed across the street at a bar called Cheers.

"Somebody just got kidnapped over there three weeks ago. Dude was coming out of the bar, and they pulled up in a van. Beat the hell out of him with a pistol. Shot him in the head two times. He *lived*. Down the street right here, a little girl got off the bus from school. Got snatched. Killed. Put under a porch. 14 years old."

"So... how does this end?"

"It doesn't."

"Not ever?"

"In this area, it's not. Because poverty is poverty. Like... shit. Who's to say we're going to wake up tomorrow? And that's how we're living. That's all it is, it's about right now," Rio continued. "If you ain't got a right now, you ain't got nothing here."

I returned inside, shaken but thankful for Rio's commitment to candor. During my high school years, I worked with the Rockford Park District's playground programs, offering free summer camps in neighborhoods across the Rockford area. I was a counselor at a playground in the suburbs in the morning and a playground in a similar area to the one surrounding Skeets in the afternoon. I loved the job which entailed playing games of dodgeball and soccer with kids outside all day, despite being told (correctly) by a camper that I "throw like a white cracker bitch" during a game of football. Those summers working with Rockford kids had a profound impact on me. Hearing stories of violence in the neighborhood from the mouths of 11-year-olds troubled me, but it hit home when one of my campers didn't return because his family had been caught in a drive-by shooting blocks from the playground at Keye-Mallquist Park. I understood what violence did to a public psyche, and I tried to imagine what constant community violence would do to someone's state of mind. If tomorrow was a question mark, why save money if you could be killed by gunfire at a stop sign? Why earn a degree when family members are found dead without justice?

Though I was distracted by what I had learned, my reappearance inside the bar did not go unnoticed. I was approached by a bartender with closely-cropped hair, Denise. She offered to show me a hand-painted mural in the backyard. I agreed. She took me by the hand and led me through the crowded bar, shouting "excuse me!" every few steps.

In the backyard, Denise stood in a leather jacket and pointed out faces in the mural of both national and local Black celebrities. Denise recounted the history of the mural with a palpable sense of pride as I recorded. She gestured to the bar.

"This is all we have. Tomorrow's not promised to any of us… it's only by the grace of God that you're gonna be here, and you should try to enjoy your life while you're here. Because we don't know how much time we have left. I would prefer to love. And that's why I love this place." Denise's voice shook with emotion. "It's all about love. All about acceptance. All about knowing that a person's going through something just like I'm going through something… and I know I can come here and release it a little."

"Just Because" by Johnnie Taylor started playing inside the bar. Someone cheered.

"Do you think if there was a Skeets in every neighborhood in the United States that we'd live in a better country?" I asked.

Denise grinned. "Yes, we would."

I thought of the occasional, isolating feeling of not having somewhere I belonged while living in the big cities. "I think a lot of people feel like they don't have a place to go like this. They don't have a place that feels like family," I said.

"And that makes me sad," she said, and she looked it. "Some people would say I'm just a bartender, but I refuse to close this place on a holiday because I know that I might have a customer who doesn't have anywhere to go. I cook every holiday. If I see someone walking down the street that might not have something, I say 'come get yourself something to eat,' because I couldn't rest, thinking someone didn't have anywhere to go or didn't have a hot meal. We're gonna feed 'em. Not just me. No, *we're* gonna feed 'em. It's what we do, baby."

As we walked inside, I told Denise that today was my first full day of the trip, and how welcome I felt despite being nervous about jumping into the unknown for the next five months.

She shook her head and shouted at me over the swelling chorus of "Just Because."

"You take this love you have here," she said pointing at my chest like she was conjuring a talisman. "You'll meet some assholes, but everything's going to be fine if you keep this love and don't you forget it."

She gave me a hug and disappeared behind the bar to greet a regular who had just walked through the door. I looked across the bar to Ram and Austin, who were laughing and clinking their glasses with a group of 70-year-old men in coveralls. There wasn't a lonely person in sight.

THE NORTHEAST

VERMONT WAS on fire as Belinda crossed the bridge over Lake Champlain, creating a perfect contrast to the cool industrial beauty of Cleveland. New England was lit by autumn colors as I sped through hills of green, gold, and crimson. Starting in the bluest region of the country was about more than the foliage, however. I was starting in my comfort zone; I had reached out to local political figures to schedule interviews. However, after my discussion with Denise and Rio, I was realizing that I was searching for something beyond simply a discussion about the policies of local government.

Before these meetings, I wanted to mingle with some locals. I drove through Burlington and pulled up to a senior center in the neighboring town of Winooski (population 7,242). It was a one-story building with a vegetable garden along the perimeter. I arrived the day after an annual pumpkin-carving festival, and the seniors were spent so the turnout was small: only four coffee-sipping septuagenarians sat at a table in the long fluorescently-lit room. There were three women—Barb, Rose, and Jan—and one man, Jasper, a French-Canadian who moved to Vermont when he was a child. They all told me that Jan was the newest addition to

Winooski, having moved there in the 1970s. Jan was a part of a senior dance troupe called the "High Steppers," which performed a mixture of line and ballroom dancing, and she told me excitedly how they were starting to get "some real recognition," as they were going to be performing for the mayor of Burlington later that day. Jan explained how the High Steppers had been a way to bridge cultural gaps between life-long Winooski residents and the influx of South Asian immigrants who had recently joined the Winooski Senior Center. The seniors had gone out of their way to make the new members feel welcome by hiring interpreters to hear their stories and enlisting the High Steppers to lead dancing classes and, in turn, learn their cultural dances well.

"They were proud, proud that we were interested," said Jan.

When the conversation turned to local politics, they told me how Vermont is famously civil and surprisingly split, with a moderate, popular Republican governor currently in office.

"There was a debate between two people for a state senate seat last week," Rose told me. "He was a Republican who played cello and she was a Democrat who played guitar. They had their debate, and then—"

"They played a duet," said Jasper, chuckling. "It was on the news."

"It was really nice to see them put their disagreements aside."

"Is this type of thing typical?" I asked, amused.

They all shrugged. "It is in Vermont."

"They should pass a law in Congress," Rose added. "Make it mandatory that after every debate, every pair of rivals has to play a duet."

"Or a two-man show."

"Or line dancing!" added Jan, the pumpkin pin on her hat bobbing as she nodded vigorously.

The idea of two people who disagreed on politics creating something together, transcending the labels of "Democrat" or "Republican" to make music, felt like something from a bygone era. It helped me understand how it was possible that Phil Scott, a Republican, could be a successful governor in the same state that elected a Democratic Socialist like Bernie Sanders. I drove east towards the most rural parts of Vermont, keen to understand Vermont's political civility and how it could be instructive for American democracy as a whole.

My next appointment was with Christine Hallquist, the first transgender gubernatorial candidate in American history, after she spoke on a panel of candidates at a town hall. When I pulled off the highway, I found myself on one long road with a Dollar Store and large town hall and discovered I was looking at pretty much the entirety of the village of Fairlee (population 983). I arrived in the large, recently renovated wooden town hall to find tables laden with cookies, donuts, and apple cider. It was almost frozen in time, with wooden chairs facing a panel decorated with red, white, and blue trappings in front of a stage accented by a mural of Lake Morey. I could imagine de Tocqueville visiting a community meeting at a hall like this in 1831. The event was being held two weeks before the 2018 midterm elections, and attendance was high. As Fairlee residents poured in, they were handed slips of paper on which to write anonymous questions for the panel. I grabbed a piece and took a seat. I had expected the event to just feature prominent Democrats, but as the candidates began their introductions, I realized that the state legislators, congressional candidates, and gubernatorial candidates were a mix of Republicans and Democrats. There was no marker of who was from which party.

One particular candidate drew my attention. She had a curtain of black hair and wore an orange blazer with a prominent gold cross around her dark-skinned neck.

"We need new leadership in Washington," 25-year-old Anya Tynio declared in a throaty, confident voice. Though she was younger than me, she was a candidate for Vermont's at-large (only)

U.S. Congressional seat. When she expressed how America has been "winning again" on national defense, something clicked into place: Anya was a Republican.

I became more and more fascinated by this candidate on a panel of people twice her age. I kept waiting for her to trip up on a question, but she deftly pivoted on climate change to the economic benefits of cutting certain toxins from industry altogether. *She's good,* I thought, remembering all of the presidential candidates and political surrogates I had seen stumping ahead of the Iowa Caucuses. A written question from the audience was addressed to her: "Who did you support in the Republican primary?"

"Donald Trump," she said unabashedly.

There were no jeers. The next question was about affordable housing.

After the panel, Christine and I discussed her time as the CEO of the Vermont Electric Cooperative, and how renewable energy and a strong business model aren't mutually exclusive.

"You make the economic argument," she said, adjusting a red scarf around her neck. "At least five of my twelve board members were Trump supporters. In Vermont, we export two billion dollars a year to the fossil fuel industry. We could keep that money in the state, grow jobs."

I asked Christine to talk about her historic campaign as a transgender woman. "Do you think the attention to that detail is exciting or distracting?"

Christine thought for a moment. "In Vermont, I'm running on the issues. I don't talk about being transgender. I infer, I say 'running for governor *isn't* the hardest thing I've ever done'," said Christine with a sly grin. "Vermonters are focused on what I'm going to do for them in terms of policy."

After I bid Christine goodbye, the organizers of the event asked us all to leave the hall.

I walked out of the hall, keeping pace with the orange-blazered woman from the panel. Anya turned to me and introduced herself.

Before I knew it, we were standing outside discussing Anya's surprising run for Congress as cars pulled out of the lot. Anya told me she had decided to run to address rural Vermont issues and finished second in the Republican primary, but when the winner had to withdraw, she became the nominee.

"If I win, I will be the first woman sent to Washington from the state of Vermont. But I want people to support me because of my policies," she said. "I think it's offensive that all women have to support another woman. I want people to vote for me because of my ideas, not my gender."

"I wasn't expecting to meet a Trump supporter in Vermont. And you definitely weren't what I expected."

"Preconceived notions are always different from reality, aren't they?" she said, smiling. She thanked me and strolled into the autumn night.

Tocqueville said, "political parties which I style great are those which cling to principles… to ideas, and not to men," and Vermont seemed to still live by these words. Though neither Anya nor Christine won their 2018 bids, I admired both women for their candor, courtesy, and decency. Pulling onto the highway, I thought of the two of them in a political matchup someday. I imagined Anya pulling out a jazz flute and Christine wheeling in a piano after a fierce debate, before playing a duet that celebrates the ability to raise their individual voices in Vermont, a state that truly listens.

The next morning, Belinda and I drove across the border into New Hampshire. I arrived at Dartmouth College in Hanover (population 11,485) in a downpour and within two seconds of getting out of the car, I was accosted by a clipboard-waving student trying to register me to vote.

"I'm not from here," I told him.

"Where *are* you from?" he asked, not believing me.

I glared at him. My lack of a stable voting address was a sore spot. I had been asked this question so many times, and it felt strange not to have a solid answer for such a core tenant of my identity.

I walked towards the cafeteria where I was meeting Max, the president of the Dartmouth College Democrats. I arrived to find a junior with messy brown hair dressed in an unassuming knit sweater carrying a tray of French fries.

I sat down with him at a cafeteria table and launched right into the difficult questions.

"How relevant do you actually feel like the College Dems are at Dartmouth?"

He didn't flinch. "I think very relevant. We've reached meme status."

A pause.

"Are you familiar with college meme groups?"

I nodded. Oxford had an active and very entertaining meme page on Facebook: The Oxford Dank Memes Society.

"Well, we're meme famous. We're the third most relevant meme on Dartmouth's campus."

I searched Max's face for some hint of a joke. There was none to be found.

Max pulled up some memes from the group "Dartmouth Memes for Cold AF Teens." The memes referencing the College Dems did indeed have over three hundred likes (roughly 10% of the student population), and most of them seemed to be in reference to the Dems harassing people on the street and spamming group chats. Basically, it seemed like the reputation of the Dartmouth College Dems was shameless.

"You have to understand, New Hampshire is the last true swing state," Max explained, still not cracking a smile. "In 2016, Hillary Clinton won the state by 2,000 votes. Our [Democratic] senator, Maggie Hassan, beat Kelly Ayotte by just over 1,000 votes. If Hassan lost, the Affordable Care Act would be dead today. Repeal failed by one vote. Dartmouth is a college of 4,400 people. Mostly liberal. You do the math."

Al Gore had lost New Hampshire in 2000 by a similarly close 7,000 votes. If Gore had won New Hampshire, he would have won the Electoral College. "So basically, Dartmouth Dems have to stay relevant any way they can because elections here are usually closer than expected," I said.

"Exactly," said Max, wildly gesticulating. "Because this stuff matters. The more they meme about us, the more we are reminding people to vote. So, if we're aggressive, we're relevant." Max continued. "If for the midterms, 20 people go out for twelve weeks and get five people a week to vote, that's a thousand extra votes. That effort essentially elected Maggie Hassan. Saved the Affordable Care Act." Finally, he smiled. "So, I would say College Dems are weirdly relevant, as demonstrated by our meme presence on campus."

Max dipped a french fry in barbecue sauce, but it felt more like he was dropping a mic.

From Hanover, I drove through the mountains and was absolutely stunned to find that at one moment Belinda was hugging the curves of a road flanked by late autumn trees and then a few thousand feet up she was battling through snow, the roads surrounded by snow-covered evergreens, only to descend into autumn again. This was New Hampshire: two seasons in five minutes. As I approached North Conway's small downtown, I had the distinct impression that the New Hampshire state of mind has a lot more to do with the outdoors than the cities.

I arrived at Frontside Coffee Roasters to meet Sarah, a wilderness guide with fiery red hair and a contemplative spirit, who was sitting in a patch of sun next to the window. When I asked her what we ought to do, she confirmed my impression that the outdoors are the real draw in North Conway (population 2,410).

"You can't visit New Hampshire and not go for a hike."

The next thing I knew, we were in her car, driving up to Cathedral Ledge, a stone lookout over a valley of reds, golds, and greens. *God*, I thought, as most Midwesterners do when they see exciting topography, *I can't believe people get to live here.* As we looked over, Sarah talked to me about her guide work with Summit Achievement, a youth outdoor therapy program for teens dealing with mental illness. She had been working for eight days on, six days off in the woods of Vermont, New Hampshire, and Maine.

"These kids struggle with all types of things, from depression and anxiety to poor self-esteem," she said, leaves crunching under her boots as we hiked towards a creek. "Something about putting kids out in nature in a different context allows them to reinvent how they see themselves."

Sarah took me to Diana's Baths, a waterfall pooling over a cratered rock formation (and originally the very wet play place for the Victorian aristocracy in their full suits and skirts.) We dipped our toes in and met some fellow hikers who had just seen a baby black bear on the trails. I decided it might be time to go.

That night, we stayed with Sarah's friends in North Conway. It was unclear who lived there or owned the apartment, because it seemed it was occupied by guides cycling in and out on the two-weeks-on/one-week-off system. I slept on the couch, but woke up in the morning to a knock on the door.

I pushed off the blanket and opened the door. Into the apartment came a tall shivering youth in a North Face coat. He immediately walked into the apartment and collapsed on the couch I had been sleeping on, shuddering violently.

Sarah and two other guides emerged from the bedroom and took one look at the intruder. "Hey Jonah! You okay?"

He stared off into space. "Just got back."

They started asking him about his expedition, but he simply gave one-word answers. They brought him out a bright orange sleeping bag. His pale hands reached out for it and slowly wrapped it around his body, hiding his face from view.

Sarah and the others hardly seemed concerned. "Anyone want a joint or a cup of tea?"

I opted for the tea and began to pack up my belongings when I heard a thud. Jonah had fully collapsed onto the floor, unmoving.

"Should he see a doctor or something?" I asked, zipping my bag.

They shook their head. "He'll be fine. Doctor's visits are so expensive, it's not really worth it."

I said goodbye to our hosts, unclear on who actually lived there. I gave the blank figure on the floor a small wave.

I pulled into Portland (population 66,882), Maine's largest city, a sea-front town of cobblestone streets and red brick buildings. I walked through the tidy streets to City Hall, where I was meeting with the mayor of Portland, Ethan Strimling. Strimling is what central casting would look for in a mayor, with wavy silver hair and a genuine grin. When I asked him a bit about his background, I discovered why my first impression was of an actor: Ethan had studied acting at Juilliard.

"*That* Juilliard?"

He laughed. "Yeah, that Juilliard."

I was genuinely fascinated. "How did politics come out of that?"

He laughed again. "My dad was an actor in New York, my grandma was an actress. So it was kind of the family business," he explained. "When I turned 19, I started to realize that acting wasn't a decision I had made. And I think the faculty at Juilliard recognized that as well, and so I kind of went up to Maine and disappeared into the woods for a year. Then I first got hooked up with a Congressman named Tom Andrews from this area, and he taught me that you can be a progressive and win."

As the actor-turned-mayor discussed affordable housing, I thought about how values of humility and collaboration—necessities in theatre—had been forgotten in government. There could be no gridlock in theatre: disagreements had to be resolved quickly under pressure to deliver a product with the fingerprints of every participant. It was also, in my experience, one of the best ways to build a community.

I drove to a tiny town called Scarborough, (population 19,922) and while driving, I got a call from Janet Mills, the woman who would in a few weeks become the first female governor of Maine. She apologized for not being able to connect, but she was campaigning way up north in the final days before the election. Because I was conscious of the fact that I hadn't been able to see much of northern Maine, I asked Janet about her hometown of Farmington (population 7,760) and the concerns of the rural parts of the state.

"In Farmington, Franklin county, we've lost mill jobs in recent years. We've lost textile jobs in recent decades. Shoe manufacturing is virtually gone. The paper industry has greatly reduced its work-force. A lot of the industries we relied on have disappeared. Franklin County *was* the largest toothpick manufacturer in the world," she said.

I thought of Rockford, "Screw City." Everything had to be made somewhere. As she listed off statistics and policies, I was thinking about my rootlessness.

"So why should I move to Maine?" I blurted out.

She paused. "Because… you will love it here," she said, adding with a chuckle, "and because we need you."

I laughed. "What do you mean you need me?"

"We need people. I don't even know how old you are, but I'm guessing as a student you're younger than 50. We need people with brain power like yourself to come to Maine. We need a younger workforce, because we have opportunities for you here, and we think… *I* think you will love it here."

. . .

Massachusetts meant traffic. Belinda and I fought through honks and glares as we sped through the underground highways under Boston (population 685,094). I spent my first night doing the local thing: watching the Red Sox play the L.A. Dodgers in the World Series at a bar near Fenway. Go figure it ended up being the longest World Series game in history, lasting a record-breaking 18-innings and ending at five in the morning. The Sox didn't even win.

The next day I went to a get-out-the-vote event with the mayor of Boston, Marty Walsh, and the touring cast of *Hamilton* in the Roxbury neighborhood. The morale was low in Boston, as it seemed everyone had stayed up to watch the World Series. I approached Marty Walsh, a tall man with a ruddy face, at the event, wondering if the mayor was as exhausted as I was as we discussed the need to refocus on local government.

"I'm part of the U.S. Conference of Mayors, a bipartisan group of mayors, and we rally around issues like climate change, like immigration, like economic development, and we don't let the national conversation cloud our judgment." He said good mayors steal ideas from each other—no matter if the idea is from a Democrat or Republican.

Outside the event, I met a young journalist waiting for the bus from Roxbury to Cambridge. He was a sophomore who was covering the event for the Tufts University student newspaper, and we chatted while standing out in the awful gusty wind and rain.

"So you want to be a journalist?"

He thought for a second. "I don't know if I'm cut out for it."

"What do you mean?"

"I feel like I don't write sensational enough stories to make it."

My umbrella blew inside out. "What do you want to write about?"

He shrugged. "Positive stories going on in the community. But all they want now is clickbait."

When he got off the bus, I was left alone scrolling through CNN. *The 64 most outrageous lines from Trump's incoherent speech to the*

NRA. Click click click. De Tocqueville had observed that the American press "displays the same violence without the same reasons for indignation" as post-revolutionary France. Maria, a classmate from Mexico City, had remarked on the American media before I left on my journey. "The news tricks people, but at the same time, it's like people allow themselves to be tricked." Maybe the question wasn't one of fake news or real news. It was the constant sensationalism that people were tired of, and the lack of any glimmer of hope or solutions to problems. We had been conditioned to expect outrage and drama.

Ten minutes later, I looked up. We were now on a bridge crossing the Charles River out of Boston and into Cambridge (population 118,977). I was on my way to meet Quentin Palfrey, a candidate for Massachusetts Lieutenant Governor, at the coordinated Democratic campaign office in Cambridge. Quentin was a Harvard-educated man in a crisp white shirt who had worked in the Obama administration. We sat down in a conference room with a map of Massachusetts on the wall.

"You've worked at the federal level and you're running for the state government now. What do you think is the role of the state government versus the federal government?"

He nodded slowly, weighing every word. "I think this is a really important question, especially in the Trump era. State governments have always been the innovators. Massachusetts in particular has been a leader. Supreme Court Justice Brandeis used to talk about the states as the laboratories of democracy."

I had never heard that phrase before, but I loved it. "Do you think the federal government should craft laws in a state-by-state approach based on this laboratory idea?"

"There are certain policies that work better at a local level, and certain kinds of policies that work better at a national level or international level," he said. I pointed out Massachusetts as the birthplace of the healthcare policy that was the model for Obamacare, ironically under Republican Governor Mitt Romney.

Quentin explained how he had played a role in implementing the 2006 healthcare reform, and adopting an existing state law into federal policy allowed for a more thorough examination of its successes and failures.

In November, Quentin and his running mate would go on to lose the election to incumbent Republican Governor Charlie Baker. Even though I had gone into the Northeast expecting a Democratic bastion, every single state I had visited thus far had Republican governors before the 2018 midterms. The idea of "laboratories of democracy" allowed states to act as case studies for different policies. Perhaps the Republican argument for more local and state control was what had won over voters. Designating priorities to different levels of government could give communities feelings of agency and allow people to refocus on local levels of government— the level that most affects their community. I thought of the emphasis on local municipal government that de Tocqueville had admired about America. Whether or not Republican governments delivered on this promise, perhaps a return to municipal participation and local control was what people were hungry for.

I consciously wanted to seek out some rural perspectives in Rhode Island, so I began in a town called Foster (population 4,606). The problem was, when my navigation told me I had arrived, I only saw a gas station at the intersection. I turned around in a driveway with a "no trespassing" sign posted above a picture of a gun and drove back to the gas station.

"Excuse me," I asked two teenage boys behind the counter. "Where's the Foster downtown?"

The boy with shaggy hair didn't smile. "This is it."

I looked outside at an unmarked building across the street. "Is that city hall?"

He shook his head. "That's a fire station."

"What do you have here?"

"Literally nothing," the other boy, baby faced and muscular, piped in.

"We just hang out in the parking lot most days."

"You have to have something," I said.

"We don't have a gym. We don't have a pool. We don't have a place to buy protein powder..."

I was already planning my exit. "Do you have a bathroom?"

The boys both looked at each other. "We don't."

After my underwhelming visit to Foster, I was more determined than ever to find a conservative perspective (and a bathroom) as I pulled into Providence (population 180,393). I texted a friend at Brown University asking if she knew any conservatives. She knew one: Brett.

Meeting Brett at Chipotle, I could immediately differentiate him from the other backpack-toting college students. Over six and a half feet tall with dark hair and features, Brett was a starting player for Brown's football team. I bought him a burrito (the negotiated price for his time), and he started talking about being a lone Trump supporter at a rabidly liberal school. I had expected him to come in swinging—instead, he mildly said that he just didn't talk much about his political beliefs anymore. However, Brett quickly became animated when the topic turned to the campus culture of activism. He discussed how when the New York Police Chief who implemented "stop and frisk" came to talk to the students, protests broke out in the auditorium, preventing anyone from hearing him or asking questions. He told another story of a transgender activist, Janet Mock, who campus protesters had prevented from speaking on transgender rights because she was being hosted by Hillel (the Jewish campus institution), even though the talk had nothing to do with the Israeli/Palestinian conflict.

"There's this liberal idea of quieting other opinions... we are Brown students. We're smart enough to listen and ask questions. To stand at the podium one by one and say 'I disagree with you, I think everything you're doing is wrong, you're a bad person, here's my question.' But that's not what they do here. They yell. They protest. Some people believe you shouldn't give certain people platforms at a place like Brown. It should be the opposite. If Brown is such a great place, the only way to learn is through conversations with different opinions."

Belinda was parked in front of a clinic in a shabbier area of Providence. As I unlocked the door, I saw a woman sitting on the stoop, her head in her hands. Something drew me to her—I circled back. Her name was Leanne. She talked about her weekly appointments to combat her anxiety and panic attacks, all the while illegally living with her terminally-ill mother in an assisted living home.

"I have no social life," she said, telling me how she had to sneak in and out of the compound because she felt the state government prioritized giving housing to people with alcohol addictions to get them off the street. "I'm homeless and need an apartment and I basically did everything I needed to do through Gateway. They'll see if I qualify for a voucher. It seems like all the alcoholics and the drunks get help and not I. I'm not an alcoholic, I don't do drugs. But they crawl up on the sidewalk near McDonalds and sleep when they have a house. People like me, I'm looking for a place to live and it's hard. It's hard," she said.

I asked her where she saw herself in five years. She looked down at her feet. 'Owning my own house."

As Belinda drove out of Providence, heavy traffic slowly turned to heavy trees and I found myself the only car on the road. The Rhode Island state of mind was perplexing me. The word that kept popping into my head as I crossed the state line was "unbalanced." The wealth of the Brown students compared to the struggles of Leanne. The urban centers of Providence and the sparseness of Foster. Rhode Island was the smallest state, but it also presented one of the biggest contrasts. I acknowledged that my impressions were based on chance encounters, but something about the stories I was hearing painted a picture of the country that was more vivid than any data or studies I had read could convey.

It was night-time when I arrived in New Haven (population 129,585), meaning that, in the darkness, I missed any nuance between Rhode Island's wooded backroads and Connecticut's wooded backroads. I met my friend Jonathan at the Yale University law student bar, a delightfully dingy downstairs room with a popcorn machine and a group of lawyers gearing up for a pub quiz. Jonathan and I had overlapped on the Hillary Clinton campaign in Iowa, but he had gone on to other western states to work in the data department. He was originally from St. Anthony, Idaho, and was still in general wonderment about ending up at Yale. This was ironic, considering Jonathan is one of the most accomplished people I had ever met. Jonathan was a Mormon who had attended Brigham Young University and done his two-year mission in Japan before he stepped outside of the Mormon community for the first time when he arrived in Sioux City, Iowa.

I watched, surprised, as Jonathan ordered a beer: he had started drinking less than a year ago after leaving the church. I sensed he was ready to move in a new direction with like-minded people.

"I'll tell you this, having left Mormonism. It was really hard for me to move outside my community and recognize I don't have a support system or a safety net. For example, I moved to New Haven and like, at other points of my life," he said, motioning to the bartender, "there'd be a Mormon church there to welcome me and help me move into my apartment. If I wanted that."

Jonathan suggested that while in Idaho I ought to talk to his dad. His father was a conservative Mormon who voted for Trump after working in a sawmill for 30 years, but was very involved with the church and the community, spending most of his free time volunteering.

"Civic engagement! That's commendable," I said. "That's why it's so messed up that Hillary called them all deplorable."

"They *are* deplorable."

I paused. "Right, maybe some of them. But not—"

"No, they are."

I changed the subject. Jonathan pulled out his phone and logged onto Grindr, and began chatting with a guy who had only an arm as a profile picture.

"If old Jonathan could see me now," he said, sipping a fresh beer.

Leaving the bar, we walked down the restaurant-lined New Haven streets. I realized I had never seen Jonathan after a few drinks before. A new directness emerged from his generally soft-spoken demeanor as he started to reprimand me for the conservatives I was hoping to talk to in future states.

"You shouldn't put rural America on a pedestal."

"I'm not going to do that."

"Because they're racist. Sexist. Homophobic. And you shouldn't be writing about them," he said, his voice strained. "The world doesn't need another *Hillbilly Elegy*."

I tried to explain that I had to keep an open mind and not instantly write anyone off, otherwise I would only be proving a preconceived hypothesis.

"Fine," he said, walking forward without another word.

We got back to his apartment and I tried to clock where things had gone wrong. I asked him for an example of sexist and racist activity where he had come from.

"My dad told my mom not to go back to school. He thinks a woman's place is in the home. She's the head of nursing now at the hospital and *still* he doesn't support my mom, even though she's the breadwinner."

"What does he think of you being gay?"

He averted his gaze to the books on his bedside table. "He doesn't know."

Jonathan looked stricken. I could understand. Even though I was privileged enough to come from a family where love was unconditional, we had our own struggles. For the first time on the trip, I told someone my story.

Boylan Central Catholic High School in Rockford was not an ideal place to be a closeted class president. When I started in 2006, the school was still run by clergy and featured most of the same administration from its opening in 1965. There was no air conditioning and the price of admission included daily religion classes, a Pro-Life club, and an underground ring of teachers who secretly identified as liberal, which I discovered after being admonished for speaking in favor of healthcare reform in class. With an acute awareness that there was more to life than the rules of Boylan Catholic, I learned when to be respectfully subversive and when to smile and remind myself this was simply a means to an end: enrollment at a liberal college. Despite my outspoken views that health care was a human right, I somehow won a plurality in a five-way race for class president my sophomore year. It was 2008 and change was coming: Obama was on track to become the first Black president, and I was suddenly finding my attraction to my male classmates was less of a reason to hate myself.

That summer during a camping trip in the Grand Canyon, I had slept under the stars next to a handsome surfer from Sacramento; when I woke up to find his arm over me in the middle of the night, something cosmic shifted within me. Whether it was a mistake or intentional, I knew something had clicked into place as I allowed myself to be held in my sleeping bag. Something that felt so epic couldn't be wrong. Back at Boylan and dealing with these exciting new feelings, 15-year-old me was starting to consider making history by coming out to force a much-needed dialogue about the stale morality we were being taught. I saw how the future was shaping up and any visibility felt important to build that future. And I've just never been good at faking things.

I was rarely dishonest, but when I was caught lying to stay the night at a friend's 18th birthday party—she was one of the few safe people I was allowed to be out to—my parents staged an intervention. They mistakenly thought I was using the party as an excuse to have sex with my on-and-off girlfriend at the time, which was ludicrous considering the situation. When confronted with the lie, I figured this was the inflection point I was waiting for; the truth would set me free: I told them about the Grand Canyon. I told them about my feelings. I told them about the party. I watched as the movie my parents thought they were in suddenly lurched into another genre. They seemed absolutely thunderstruck—I thought my childhood obsession with the Wicked Witch of the West had been enough of a warning.

When my Dad picked me up from school the next day, he looked brittle behind the wheel of his sedan. I got in the car, trying to suss out his mood

"In this family, we'll love you no matter what," he said, looking at me intently. "But I'm scared to think that my son is joining the most hated group of people on earth."

In that moment, I had an inkling that he was wrong. I knew that things were changing. But it was also the first time I saw anything resembling a shadow of fear from my father about my future. And strangely, despite my father saying something I knew to be untrue, I felt loved.

We drove around for two hours. For the first time, my dad brought someone else into the equation: my brother. Soon my little brother would be attending my very same high school.

"Isn't it unfair to him? Setting him up to be bullied off the bat for something outside of his control?"

"But what if I'm right? What if no one cares? What if I can—"

"Can what?"

I gazed out the window. "I don't know, change people?"

He looked out the window, thinking. Finally he spoke. "You're so..."

The suspense filled the car, as my brain began to play the ultimate game of paternal-approval Mad Libs. So brave? Idealistic? Honest?

"... young." he said. "Wait until college. Enjoy your high school experience. Don't make it harder on yourself."

"But this isn't about me enjoying myself, Dad," I replied. "It's about being honest among all of the bullshit they tell us in school." The hypocrisy, more than anything, was the driving force behind my quest to be honest, and in a society that claimed to value honesty, I didn't understand how this was the wrong thing to do.

"I agree." From my dad, a Christian, this was a big statement. "But... is it worth hurting your brother to fight a battle you're probably going to lose?"

My brother Andrew was probably my best friend in the entire world; we had diametrically opposed interests but a nearly identical sense of humor. The thought of his high school experience— something that was difficult regardless—being complicated by my actions would be more than I could stomach. By the time I woke up the next morning, this argument won out within me. I told my parents we wouldn't discuss what had happened until I was 18 and we could go back to the way things were, or pretend we could anyway.

This small act of sacrifice is something I look back on with mingled regret and pride. My drive to be honest and become a role model in my small, conservative town ultimately was trumped by the loyalty I felt to my family. I wanted to see them happy and my wishes to be a provocateur were always less potent than protecting the people I loved. But then again, this self-martyrdom may have also simply been an excellent way to cover up the fact that I was scared.

I don't blame my parents for trying to give me an "easy life" at the expense of authenticity. Conversely, in seeing me struggle, my parents became more empathetic to other walks of life. I understood that my optimism stemmed from how my family affected each other for the better, but I knew that it would be naive to assume that Jonathan's father would surprise him with the same support.

He nodded, his storm seemingly quelled after listening to my story. "I went to BYU. I knew I was gay. I would wake up every morning and cry in the shower. This went on for *years*. Now that I came out, things are better. I mean, it's still life, but…"

I understood. The Hillary campaign was the first place that he had ever felt fully accepted for who he was. Yale had allowed him to experience things that had been explicitly forbidden at home.

"I wish gay people went to places like Idaho, so kids could have an example. So they don't have to feel alone like you did."

Jonathan smiled slightly. "That's what I wrote my Yale essay about."

"Being an example?"

"Yeah," he said, looking off into the distance. "If even one gay Mormon kid could see what I had done, and know it's possible… this will all have been worth it."

While I had been considering a return to the heartland as a solution to some of democracy's problems, for some, like Jonathan, the inverse was what he needed. He had to come to Yale to find acceptance and fulfill his potential. We had found common ground, but my positive outlook didn't mean conservative America didn't leave scars on those who had to live there and fight quiet battles on their own.

I'll never forget where I was on December 14, 2012: 20 dead children, 6 dead teachers, and Obama's single tear are forever seared into my memory. Driving west through rural Connecticut, I knew that a visit to Newtown (population 27,560) was necessary.

I arrived at Sandy Hook Elementary School. Walking onto the campus, I noticed how peaceful it was. The trees swayed in the wind, casting shadows on the empty parking lot below. The entire school had been recently rebuilt, constructed of a warm wood exterior that matched the surrounding forests. I was glad it was a Saturday, and I could be alone without observation as I walked around the campus, looking for a memorial where I could pay my respects. I was moved by the peacefulness of the small wooded school in a sleepy little town, contrasted with the senseless violence that had occurred over six years ago. After 40 minutes of searching, I found no memorial. I felt ashamed at my feeling of incompleteness, as if I was only looking for catharsis. Driving towards town, I passed a sign advertising a spaghetti supper at the Methodist Church. The confusion of my visit to the school compelled me to go inside.

In the church basement, I paid $10 for mediocre spaghetti (*without* meatballs). I was eyeing the room for a place to scarf down my food when I heard someone addressing the woman ahead of me in line.

"Thanks so much for your work, Pastor Lori."

My ears perked up. I realized I was standing in line behind the pastor of the church, a short woman with gray hair and a warm smile. When I introduced myself and told her about my project, Pastor Lori invited me to join her and her husband John for dinner.

They had moved to Sandy Hook in 2015. Lori described her arrival to the church as offering "a clean slate." I told them about my visit to the school and expressed my surprise by the lack of any sort of memorial to commemorate the 2012 shooting. She told me that she was surprised too, arriving in the aftermath of a tragedy, to find the community divided between two factions: one that wanted to remember and pay homage to the tragedy that happened in their midst, and the other that wanted to move on from the horror and make Sandy Hook something other than the location of a nationally observed shooting.

"There's a memorial service every December 14th, and this year didn't have the same intensity as last year... so that might mean that there's been some sort of healing."

Her husband gesticulated over his spaghetti with a fork.

"People want Sandy Hook to be more than just what happened in 2012."

"Which was hard for us to understand at first," she said, opening her mouth, then hesitating. "A little bit of personal sharing… John and I raised two sons. We lost our youngest son very suddenly in July. We've found that the folks in this church almost viscerally knew how to be with us."

"We're just starting to get out of it now," said John.

"There are days when we can, you know, live," she agreed.

The church basement buzzed around us with the click of metal forks on porcelain plates. A woman came around and refilled my plastic cup of root beer. As I watched her walk away, Lori broke the silence.

"You know, as a woman of faith, I don't believe in coincidence. It's the movement of spirit, it's God, it's the universe. Whatever language you want to give to it." Lori looked at her husband, who gave her a reciprocal, complicated smile. "As our Buddhist friend says, everything is connected… and nothing is lost."

I got back into Belinda thinking about faith. The crisis of faith in faith itself, demonstrated by Jonathan, and the need for faith in a grieving community, demonstrated by Lori and the rest of Sandy Hook. My own beliefs had always been about wading into the mystery of faith and constantly—and sometimes inorganically— trying to find a glimmer of hope. However, I was aware of the disingenuousness of how institutionalized faith tended to push away people like Jonathan in a time when community was probably needed most. In a time when there was a loss of faith in democracy itself, politics didn't seem to be enough. We needed an inclusive spiritual awakening in America, but churches weren't welcoming everyone.

Ironically, the closest I've ever felt to God was as a 19-year-old, when—at my father's request—I sat with my Lutheran pastor and told him I wasn't sure if I believed.

"I can't tell you for certain God is real," Pastor Troy responded, shrugging. "The only thing I can tell you for certain is that in my life, living by the principles of service, working with the homeless, fighting for women clergy, fighting for gay rights, and fighting to help people find meaning, I've found meaning and felt closer to God."

I still struggle with faith, especially when I see people like Jonathan rejected by theirs and pastors using their positions to fan the flames of division. But for me, having faith in a higher meaning is like having faith in the inherent goodness of people: it's a choice.

I felt the pull of New York City, my most recent American home, even as I drove down the deserted streets of Trenton, New Jersey (the capital, population 84,964) and past the boarded-up capitol building. I was on my way to have a conversation with former Republican governor Christine Todd Whitman, who had served as Governor from 1994-2001 until she became the Head of the Environmental Protection Agency under George W. Bush. But the G.O.P. had changed: Whitman, a commanding woman with a sharp smile, had very little positive to say about the state of the Republican Party.

As a self-described "Eisenhower Republican," Christine began the interview by saying that Republicans, "need the people who are in the center to try to take back the party." I agreed that the hostage-taking methods were counterproductive to democracy, and Whitman said that "what Republican moderates need to do is be a little more aggressive and be willing to take on some of the far-right." She talked about the Problem-Solvers Caucus in Congress, a bipartisan group of legislators coming up with commonsense consensus solutions to issues. Whitman reminded me that it wasn't necessarily Republicans whom I needed to talk to. "I have maintained from the very beginning that Bernie Sanders and Donald Trump voters were two sides of the same coin. They were people who were frustrated and angry that Congress wasn't doing its job; they were scared about the future." I realized that so far I had been playing it safe. Sooner or later I was going to have to talk to a Republican who was a fervent Trump supporter, not just reluctant Trump voters.

I made a quick pit stop in Princeton (population 31,386). I decided to walk through the Princeton campus. The sky was a steely gray, and the orange-brown leaves had freshly fallen. I spotted the campus cathedral and made my way inside. Chaotic music was echoing off the dimly lit stone walls. The source was the grand pipe organ over the altar, its stormy gray pipes blaring low and high melodies simultaneously. The cacophony perfectly matched how I was feeling at the moment. I had had so many experiences in such a short space of time, and I took the moment to feel overwhelmed. Something about this month, the slew of engagements in my news feeds, the sharing of professional successes, new houses made me feel as though perhaps this dream trip was occurring at the expense of advancing my life in more tangible ways. Still, I had no idea what I was supposed to do with the things I was really passionate about, or where I was meant to live, so I accepted that this trip was the thing to be done.

I met a friend, Peter, and his wife Janet for a drink at the Princeton Tap Room. Peter was a lawyer in his late 50s whom I had met at a playwriting conference at Kenyon College. Peter had recently written an article on the history of the small pub. The most interesting part of the room was the wall, where, frozen in time, hung black and white photographs of some of Princeton's most notable alumni. I looked with interest at the twenty-two-year-old faces of some of the most recognizable people on the planet. Michelle Obama. Jeff Bezos. Elena Kagan. Donald Rumsfeld. Ralph Nader. Sonia Sotamayor. Their faces were frozen in different expressions. Elena Kagan, hope. Donald Rumsfeld, self-assurance. Ralph Nadar, youthful resolve.

"You really never know what you're going to become, huh?" Peter said, looking at the wall with interest.

I nodded, haunted by the impact of the faces in front of me. The 2000 election. The Iraq War. The rise of Amazon. All of them here, frozen in time, their faces full of youthful potential. Something about it made me shiver.

"You kind of wonder if they knew where life was going to take them," I said, more to myself than to Peter.

I drove through horrendous New Jersey traffic on the turnpike to New York City (population 8,398,748), a place where you never knew what would happen next. During my time in the city, I found myself working as a playwright, a teacher at a Bronx high school, and the only white guy at a Dominican sushi restaurant in Harlem, where I was affectionately referred to as *"ojos verdes."* While the dilapidated, delayed subway system just about drove me out of the city, the MTA was nothing compared to driving around the lawless streets. Belinda swerved furiously out of the way of a taxi, then squeezed between an unloading truck and a van, and only when we passed through Chinatown and over the Brooklyn Bridge did I exhale. I parked Belinda at a cheap lot in Brooklyn and promised her I would never drive in NYC again.

I was back to see the opening of a play I wrote that was being produced at Cherry Lane Theatre. I had been given the commission to write about the First Amendment and had written a script called *Bad Press* that lampooned the 24-hour news media's malpractice during presidential campaigns. My dad, who had always implored me to keep doing theatre because it gave the family a reason to get together, had come into town with my mom and their best friends, Dave and Sara. I was only three stops on the subway towards Midtown when the disembodied MTA voice announced major delays between Brooklyn and Manhattan. Frustrated, I left the subway to catch a cab, walking next to a grumbling Chinese woman in a raincoat. As we ascended the escalator, I overheard her pick up a phone call.

"Of course I'm voting Tuesday. *Of course* I'm voting Republican."

I was late, but I also knew I had found a unicorn: a New York City Republican. I approached her and asked for an interview and discovered that she was an immigrant and a registered Republican. As frustrated MTA riders elbowed past us, Helen told me the story of her decades-long struggle getting into the USA. "I went through the legal immigration process. It was so hard to get into America. I had to wait overnight in Arlington, Virginia for my green card in the November weather; it was bitter cold. I met my husband there, in the immigration line."

"That was lucky."

"No kidding. Coming to America and being an American citizen is a big deal. If you don't know how to obey a law, you don't deserve to be a citizen. America should have a merit-based system."

"So you're a Republican because of immigration?"

She told me she was a former Democrat and had voted for Bill Clinton but hated the "reductive" Democratic party. "Women are all individual thinkers, they don't think like a block. The whole thing about identity politics… you can't do that to people. And I used to like Chris Matthews. Bill Maher, I thought he was funny. After Trump became president, all those people lost their brains. And they don't have a sense of humor anymore."

Walking to meet my family for dinner, I remembered another brush with a New York Republican. In the December after the 2016 election, one of my college friends had invited a group to her family Christmas party on Long Island. There, we were absolutely stunned to find Sean Hannity, conservative FOX news pundit and Trump whisperer, in attendance. Early in the night, he approached the group of us, saying he bet we all voted for Hillary, but we had no idea how much we were going to "be winning again" as a country under Trump.

Once the party was underway, my goal had been to track the FOX host down and ask him what he thought the Clinton campaign had missed. I stood at the bar in the basement, devising a plan to approach, when a middle-aged woman with dark hair came up to the bar and started making a drink.

"You seem deep in thought," she said, eying me.

"I'm trying to figure out if Sean Hannity would want to talk to me," I said. "I worked on the Hillary campaign."

"I bet he would."

"You think?"

"I know he would. I'm his wife."

Jill Hannity and I chatted for a bit, before she grabbed me by the arm and marched me up to her husband.

"Sean, you need to talk to this young man. He worked on the Clinton campaign and I think you'd really hit it off."

As Jill left us, I looked into Sean's face. His expression was open, quizzical almost. I was about to make my opening remarks, when I felt a girl in a velvet dress dart past me to point a finger in Sean Hannity's face.

"STANDING ROCK! Why don't you support Standing Rock?"

Brittney, a well meaning but intoxicated college friend, was now nose-to-nose with Sean Hannity, yelling at him about the construction of the Dakota Access Pipeline on the Standing Rock Indian Reservation. Hannity, shaken, began yelling back at her.

"We're going to start winning again! Just you watch!"

"STANDING ROCK!"

"Winning again!"

"But what about STANDING ROCK??"

"Winning again!"

As I tried to calm down the situation, Sean Hannity leaned into me and motioned to Brittney. "Wow, you've got yourself a little firecracker here."

Brittney's face contorted with rage. "I'm not his little firecracker, he's GAY!"

The entire party of Long Island Republicans fell silent. Sean looked at me, wide-eyed, and mumbled "yes, I guess that would be a problem," and scurried away. He avoided me for the rest of the night.

If this wasn't a crystallization of modern political dialogue, I didn't know what was.

I met my parents at an Italian restaurant in Midtown with Dave and Sara. I'm lucky to be close with my parents and their friends; they're the types whom you have one drink with and the next thing you know, you're riding a mechanical bull in Midtown.

Over pumpkin ravioli, they asked what I was learning on the trip. It seemed impossible to articulate. How could I explain over one dinner the nuances of the duet-playing politicians in Vermont, the progressive mayor in rural Ohio, a pastor of a grieving community in Connecticut? With the most recent development on my mind, I told them about Helen.

"I don't understand how any woman or immigrant could support that man," Sara said, brow furrowed. "I can't believe the hate he's unleashing. Even in Rockford…"

"What happened in Rockford?"

Dave looked grim. "Someone painted swastikas on the Coronado Theater."

The Coronado is a 1920s movie theater in the heart of downtown Rockford which had drawn crowds for the likes of Bob Dylan, JFK, and Judy Garland over the years.

"Swastikas?" I repeated, burning. Dave and Sara were Jewish. Sara softened, seeing my utter incomprehension of it all. A Jewish Brown University student supported Trump because he was pro-Israel, yet in Rockford someone was painting swastikas on a Nationally Registered Historic Landmark. Why? How?

I arrived at Cherry Lane Theatre in Soho and found my favorite people in New York gathered outside the theatre: friends from college, friends from high school, friends from the campaign, friends from the theatre scene. The familiarity washed over me. The New York state of mind was about giving anyone and everyone a place to belong. The sense of community was strong in New York in that off-Broadway playhouse, but I felt a tinge of guilt. For me, theatre had always been more about building a community. I thought of New American Theatre, where I met Rockfordians from all walks of life and befriended out-of-town actors who became my community, sitting closed in my hometown. As much as I was enjoying *Bad Press*, I recognized it was just another play in a theatre city. In New York, the theatre world would still spin, with or without me.

Afterwards, sitting at Dive Bar with my friends, Kate, a wry comedian, asked me about the moment I felt most out of my comfort zone on the trip.

"Well, I was probably one of the first white guys to walk into a bar in East Cleveland."

Morgan, a Wisconsinite who had worked in Cleveland during 2016, rolled his eyes. "*Okay,* Ryan. Which bar?"

"Skeets?"

"You went to *Skeets*?" he said, incredulous.

"Did you talk to any huge Trumpers?"

I thought about this. "Not… *huge* Trumpers."

Morgan took a sip of beer. "It's too bad you already went to Cleveland."

"Why's that?"

"Trump's doing a rally."

"When?"

"Two days from now."

I wouldn't go. I couldn't go. "Should I go?"

Morgan shrugged. "*I* would never go. But it would probably be the most culturally significant event you'll attend in your lifetime."

"I shouldn't..."

"How many times are you going to write a book about driving through the country in the middle of an election cycle?" asked Kate, deadpan.

Walking back to my parents' hotel, I passed a souvenir shop in Times Square. Even though it was past midnight, the door was wide open to coax in drunk tourists. As I walked past, something red in the window caught my eye. A stack of "Make America Great Again" hats. Here was a sign so obvious, I felt the decision had already been made for me. I had to follow the flow of the journey. I took a deep breath and walked into the store.

THE RALLY

IF THIS BOOK WERE A MOVIE, being unmasked as a Hillary staffer at a Trump rally would be my record scratch moment. Surrounded by angry, surprised Trump supporters, the scene would freeze, and I would turn to the camera in a MAGA hat: "I bet you're wondering how I got here."

On the day of the rally, I stood in Austin's Cleveland apartment gazing in the mirror like an actor in a costume fitting. I was amazed at how one red hat could completely re-contextualize my attributes. My beard, leather jacket, and unshakable Midwestern-ness were suddenly transformed into something new.

Austin walked in, tying his tie for an early morning broadcast. "Whoa."

I turned around. "Do I look convincing?"

He nodded, surprised. "Actually, yes."

I looked in the mirror again. I definitely wouldn't want to mess with the guy looking back at me.

Austin cinched his tie. "Oh, just a heads up. Just got word that someone called in a bomb threat for the rally. Be careful."

Great. If the Trump supporters didn't get me, a bomb would.

The rally was held at an airplane hangar on the day before the 2018 midterm elections. I arrived wearing my MAGA hat and a leather jacket and flannel. At this point, I was nine states in out of 50, and I knew that talking to the millions of Donald Trump voters was necessary to get the pulse of the country. Yet, sitting in the car, the weight of the event struck me. People got hit at these rallies. Journalists got heckled. All by people in the same red hat I was wearing.

When de Tocqueville visited the United States in 1831, he was floored by Americans' commitment to and participation in this new democratic form of government, a system he envied after the bloodshed and inequality of the short-lived revolutions in his native France. Democracy was an equalizer, a divine form of government that corrected the feudal and monarchic power concentrations of the past and allowed for opportunity based on merit rather than class. Someone like Trump, whose disregard for our democratic institutions and norms was a draw for many, seemed to highlight that these systems were failing us.

Of course, it was 2018. I admit I was skeptical of warnings from friends about Trump's authoritarian reflexes. I found that Democrats often overplayed their hand, seeming to oppose him at every turn and turning to hysterics (before things got truly terrifying). The knee-jerk opposition to Trump led the right to dig their heels in more, and Trump used this division to his advantage. Divide and conquer. Two years later, of course, the two camps were trained to live in different realities, denying the same set of facts about the upcoming pandemic and 2020 election. If I had known the violence and derangement that his baseless election lies would lead to, I don't think I would've made the 8-hour drive back for the rally. Everyone has their breaking point. Mine was disparaging the democracy I had spent 50 states traveling to research. I now think about Trump the way I think about asbestos; something that people thought was a strong, revolutionary solution that in hindsight was poisoning us.

Walking through the parking lot, a reporter stopped me and asked if he could interview me about my support for Trump.

I was confused, momentarily forgetting I *was* a Trump supporter from his vantage point.

"Oh!" I said, remembering. "I'm kind of here... undercover."

The reporter raised his eyebrows. "You really look the part."

I was amazed. Who said being a theatre major didn't get me anywhere?

I got to the end of the line around the same time as a group three of 40-something women and a bearded man in a MAGA hat. They were talking amongst themselves as a vendor approached to peddle Trump t-shirts. Wanting to ironically buy some Crooked Hillary paraphernalia for my campaign friends, I asked if the man had any "Hillary for Prison" shirts. He didn't, but the group in front of me laughed and turned around.

"You can get them on Amazon," said a tall lady with star-spangled leggings and flip-flops, deadly serious. "My son wore a 'Hillary for Prison' shirt to high school on election day and they knew better than to say anything."

The group laughed. I felt a twinge of annoyance. "Hillary for Prison" was only okay when I said it—for me, it was a coping mechanism to deal with the fact that the President threatened to lock up his political opponent like a dictator in a third-world country.

"Are you here alone, honey?"

"Yeah."

"Where did you come from?"

"New York," I said.

"New York? Is this your first rally?"

"Yeah." I was afraid of saying too much.

They looked at me seriously. "You're not a liberal in disguise are you?"

I waited for them to laugh. They didn't. I blanched, but then recovered.

"I'm a former liberal," I improvised with a nervous laugh. "My friends are really mad that I'm here. They think Trump supporters are all bad."

"Oh no, honey," said Chrissy. "You won't find any hate in there, it's all love."

"It's all about love," agreed Anne.

I noticed the t-shirt of the man behind her: "Hillary Sucks But Not Like Monica." All about love indeed.

I wanted to test my methodology of keeping an open mind, but I felt I needed to continue the ruse. "Yeah, all of my friends are really liberal. I'm actually doing interviews, trying to show them a different side of Trump supporters they don't see on the news."

They agreed to let me record them. Hal, a barber, started talking about the #WalkAway movement. "It was started by a gay hairdresser in New York who led a movement out of the Democratic party!"

"We love gay people," DeeDee added. (Never mind that the official Republican platform still calls for banning gay marriage.)

"Yeah," Hal agreed. "It's a movement for people who finally opened their eyes and saw the Democrats for what they are: hypocrites."

"DeeDee is a former Democrat," said Anne, pointing to DeeDee with a smirk.

"I voted for Clinton *once!*"

I found out that two in the group were veterans, as they talked vaguely about how thrilled they were with Trump's reforms to the VA. Fifteen minutes passed, and our conversation turned to talking about Trump and the media. "They take everything he says out of context."

I found myself feeling a begrudging sense of agreement. I had spent a lot of 2015 watching Trump rallies on the internet during the Hillary campaign, trying to understand the movement. While I didn't agree with a lot of what he said and found much of it to be irresponsible hyperbole, I was always surprised by the quotes the media chose to highlight. They did the public a disservice by underestimating the man, portraying him as a buffoon rather than an actual political force. After bashing on the corporate media for a little bit (I didn't find it hard to join in), they all started taking pictures together. They motioned to me, inviting me into the picture. Ah, why not?

They looked down at the picture, squealing with delight at their pink Trump hats and sweatshirts. Anne asked if I was on Facebook. I didn't want to be suspicious, so I decided to be honest. "Yep," I said. "Ryan Bernsten."

I hadn't used Facebook much in recent years, but I realized as Anne started to search for me that my most recent place of employment is still listed as "Hillary for Iowa."

Shit. Shit shit shit. I was the liberal in disguise that they were afraid of. The cat was out of the bag. There was going to be a commotion. I was going to be dissed, punched, kicked out of the rally. I saw my name come up as Anne's eyes under her pink "Women for Trump" hat narrowed.

"I need to tell you guys something, but you can't judge me," I said.

"We're conservatives, we judge everybody," Sal said wryly.

DeeDee spoke first. "You *are* a liberal in disguise."

I shook my head. "I used to work for Hillary."

A pause. "Did you really?"

"But I'm here to talk to people who voted differently" I stammered, "to try to understand people, beyond what's on the news."

Silence. They all stared at me. I was an antelope spotted by a pack of hyenas. Nobody wanted to make the first move.

Suddenly, Chrissy made a move toward me, arms outstretched. I flinched. Next thing I knew, she was pulling me into a tight hug. "God love ya," she said, "I think it's amazing that you're here."

"Welcome!"

I was suddenly surrounded by hugs from three women who could've been my mom. Hal gave me a fist bump.

Anne looked at me very seriously. "Stick with us. We're going to show you all the love here that you won't see on TV."

Bewildered, I was led by the arm into the sprawling hangar, past security who nodded at me, not checking for tickets. We got our spots in the already swelling crowd a little before noon. Trump wasn't set to arrive until after 3, so I spent the following hours with Chrissy, Anne, DeeDee, and Hal.

They didn't treat me any differently now that they knew my secret. They chatted to me about their jobs. DeeDee was a realtor, Hal was a barber. All of them loved Cleveland. I probed them on policy, waiting for an opportunity to give them the education I thought I would be able to offer. Instead, they ended up pivoting to things I knew little about: the military, the Veterans Administration, and the local economy.

"What he's done for veterans is amazing," said Hal. "All the vets I know are getting A+ treatment."

"There are 'help wanted' signs all over Cleveland," said Chrissy.

"My son is going to be an electrician," said DeeDee. "We've got a family friend who is going to get him all trained up. It's a good living, but there aren't enough skilled workers to fit the demand. Too many kids are going to college and ignoring the good-paying jobs that are out there."

I nodded. "I studied theatre in college."

"How did that work out? Are you on Broadway?"

I looked at her, surprised by her bluntness. "Nope," I said before starting to laugh.

"You should be an electrician," she said, joining me in laughing.

"I'd make a hell of a lot more money than I am now!"

As we laughed, I caught myself. I remembered that not everyone can feel safe at a Trump rally. There's evidence to suggest that not everyone *would* be safe at a Trump rally. Either way, they made an effort to point out friends of color in the crowd, from a flamboyant Puerto Rican man to an older Black woman. The

Caucasians were the definite majority, but I picked out the splashes of color and the various Hasidic Jews in full dress. The pre-rally music featured such tunes as "Macho Man" and "Memory" from *Cats*. I wondered how any homophobe could take themselves seriously in here. The event staff entertained the masses, flinging t-shirts into the cheering crowds. It reminded me of half-time at college basketball games. An older woman with a kind face behind us waved her hands for a shirt. I smiled in spite of myself. She saw me.

"If I get one I'll give it to you. My grandkids already don't talk to me because they saw a picture of me wearing one on Facebook."

DeeDee looked over. "Your grandkids?"

The woman nodded. "And their mom."

DeeDee looked grim. "My best friend from childhood just stopped talking to me out of the blue last year."

"Really?"

"Mhm. Wouldn't take my calls. Blocked me on Facebook. Blocked me on Instagram. It took me getting in touch with her mom to find out that she 'couldn't take the hate.' We used to agree to disagree about politics. There was no problem. I watched her special needs kids for free every week. That's hate?"

"It's a relief being here isn't it? No one's judging you because you don't like Crooked Hillary!"

I laughed.

"Did you hear that she's thinking of running again?" the older woman said, shaking her head.

"If she does, she's crazy," I added.

"Oh she's crazy alright," drawled a voice behind us. Two 20-something girls with baggy sweatshirts who looked like they had just rolled out of bed stood behind us. "Her and Bill. They're sick. Child prostitution. Sex slavery. The Clinton Foundation."

The three of us turned away.

"You'll see. There's big news about to come out. You'll see the truth about the Clintons. Sex trafficking."

The older woman turned to them, and said with the severity of a grandmother, "We disagree with her politics. That's all."

Cowed by the lack of commiseration, the two youths slunk back into the crowd. I was reminded just how much of this movement was fueled by conspiracy and hoped the stern grandma was the one with more influence in the MAGA world.

Before we knew it, it was ten to three. Five to three. And right on the dot, there he was. Golden hair coiffed, impressive in person. Face less orange than on-camera. Mouth pulled to one side in a self-assured smirk. Hands slowly clapping. Long red tie. Loose-fitting suit. This was him. The man who shocked the world.

It was off-putting, but I found myself whipped up by the excitement of the crowd around me. The grandma behind me was screaming. Trump said some empty words, repeating his rallying cries about the caravans on the Southern border, but his intention seemed to be more about energizing the crowd. He talked about the prosperity unlocked by the current administration, and the general incompetence of the Democrats. "If the radical Democrats take power, they will take a wrecking ball to our economy and to our future, a wrecking ball." Trump was off-the-cuff, telling us, "I used to work in Ohio for summers... I loved it. I loved it. And I won't tell you, but I used to—I shouldn't say that in this room—but I on occasion would be known to sneak into Kentucky because I liked Kentucky. I liked Kentucky for all the wrong reasons," only to find out from Hal that the drinking age was lower in Kentucky when young Donald was there.

"He's just a regular guy!" said Hal.

"He doesn't drink!" I said over fresh applause.

The Hassidic Jewish men standing near the stage were smiling and clapping. I thought of my hometown of Rockford, Illinois, where swastikas had been painted on our beautiful downtown theater. Trump had unleashed something in the hateful people across America, but I believed that the people I met neither held those beliefs nor would be capable of that. People voted for Trump for myriad reasons, and the "big tent" he had created included all types of people, from folks a lot like the people I grew up with in Rockford to believers in dangerous conspiracy theories. If my mission was to find reasonable people among the red hats, I felt I had succeeded. I was never going to change their minds by criticizing. In fact, it seemed to only anger them.

My MAGA gang invited me to a bar to hang out. I really wanted to, but I felt like I had such a complete experience that I didn't want to try my luck. I said goodbye. The women said that they would check in with me later that night on Facebook to make sure I got home safe (and they did). I was glad I met them, truly. I'm still friends on Facebook with them to this day; occasionally they'll post a meme about Hillary that will make me laugh, but mostly I've been sad to see how they continue to believe in Q-Anon and post unhinged lies about the 2020 election or the COVID vaccine. Their more caustic posts have gotten progressively less likes over the years, and it's strange to see them sporadically separated by pictures from family events or posts to commemorate lost family members. The human side could coexist with the extremist views, but it's hard to reconcile the two versions of the people I met. Still, I never feel they are entirely to blame for spouting beliefs that came from the top and trickled down to them. Someone they looked up to gave them permission to act this way and social media had, like it had for many of us, warped their perspectives.

I went to the car and put a story on my Instagram and sent out a couple of tweets telling my friends that I had survived the rally, met good people (and a couple of conspiracy theorists), but I was unharmed and even had a good time.

The next 24 hours were like something I never would have imagined. Every 30 minutes it seemed I was getting a new message, either thanking me for being open-minded or telling me that I was normalizing racism, sexism, and homophobia. One girl I knew from college sent me a long message, telling me that as a "WHITE, cis man, to them a passing guy sexuality wise" I had "minimized and normalized the hate rhetoric" and that I was a "moron."

I found this all a bit rich, seeing as this person was raised in the most affluent parts of the east coast, schooled at Northwestern, and lived in the cushiest part of Los Angeles, but I acquiesced. I deleted my posts.

Driving back from the rally, even with the outpouring of support, I was being criticized by people from different departments of my life. I started to wonder if their thoughts represented a consensus among my liberal peers. I was accused of normalizing racism by five people. All of them were white.

Thus far, my only concern had been accumulating massive debt on the trip. Now, I wasn't just afraid for my financial standing. I was afraid for my social standing too. I felt a surprising pang of sympathy for those on both sides of the aisle whose friends and family called them a "stupid liberal" or a "deplorable." I was starting to realize that the root of most political problems started with being misunderstood. While leaders in both parties aim to whip people up in their own camps, recently it had been deliberately taken to a new level. We had been taught to view each other as enemies, and as a result, it trickled down into something ugly in our communities. Politics, a necessary evil, had become synonymous with values. And friendships, families, and relationships had been ruptured as a result. The disarming power of seeing where people were coming from was an under-utilized one, and necessary before we could we set our sights on the real issues facing us: corruption, money in politics, outrage-stoking. I was thinking of a famous quote about appealing to our better angels being crucial in a democracy. I looked it up, wanting to remember it fully.

"We are not enemies, but friends. We must not be enemies. Though passion may have strained, it must not break our bonds of affection. The mystic chords of memory will swell when again touched, as surely they will be, by the better angels of our nature."

The writer was Lincoln.

THE RUST BELT

THE RUST BELT isn't so much a physical place; it's more a state of mind. For a Rust Belt native, you know it when you see it. Struggling place, Rust Belt. Closed factories, Rust Belt. Overlooked by the rest of the United States, Rust Belt. But defining the Rust Belt as a geographical region was proving elusive. I had never explored the etymology of the phrase, and I was surprised to find that it wasn't that old. Presidential candidate Walter Mondale had coined the phrase in a campaign speech in 1984, decrying how Reagan's policies were "turning our industrial Midwest into a rust bowl," and the media decided that "Rust Belt" had a better ring to it. Various maps show different Rust Belts: some include only Michigan, Wisconsin, and Pennsylvania, but others also include West Virginia, Kentucky, and Indiana, while excluding Wisconsin. Anne Trubeck articulated the dilemma of defining the region in *Time Magazine*. "Definitions of where, exactly, the Rust Belt is are also often debated. There is no answer... but in the end, anywhere an economy was previously based on manufacturing and has since been losing population can be part of the gang." My personal criteria for Rust Belt was simple: does this place feel like home?

. . .

It was election day as Belinda and I arrived at a coordinated Democratic campaign office in West Deer Township (population 11,771) outside of Pittsburgh, Pennsylvania. I collected a walk packet, drove to my designated neighborhood, and went door-to-door to remind everyone to vote in the midterm elections. I can't say I made much of a difference in that sleepy middle-class neighborhood. The lawns, crimson with fallen leaves, were all marked with reliably blue yard signs. Most of the people who weren't at work had already voted or seemed offended that I didn't trust them to do so.

Still, I posted photos of me with my clipboard doing the trendy Democratic legwork on Instagram as penance. Even though I needed social media to connect with people for nuanced, in-person conversations, complex political ideas didn't translate well to 240 characters or 15-second Instagram stories. It was my fault for trying to simplify a multifaceted experience into a format that left no room for nuance.

I drove to Erie (population 97,369), a Rust Belt town on the shores of Lake Erie. James Fallows, editor of *The Atlantic,* published an article titled "The American Dream Is Still Alive—Just Look at Erie, Pennsylvania" three months before Donald Trump won Erie County, a district that had voted for Obama twice by nearly 20-point margins. Fallows struck a hopeful tone in his article, describing a town "whose urban landscape clearly shows the structural and human marks of traumatic change, people are also trying to anticipate and adapt to those changes, to improve their individual and collective futures, and generally to behave as if they are actors in their own dramas, rather than just being acted-upon." Trump visited Erie in 2016 and railed against globalism in a town that had experienced many of its effects. He correctly predicted he would win Erie by a wide margin because "people are tired of lies, they're tired of losing their jobs, they're tired of seeing their companies being ripped out and going to other places. They're tired of China coming in and dropping steel all over the place to put your companies out of business." I wanted to see which version of Erie I experienced: the hopeful one presented by Fallows or the more apocalyptic one portrayed by Trump. I parked Belinda in the town square and walked around downtown, eventually migrating towards two people sitting on the hood of a sedan in a McDonald's parking lot. She was a Black woman in her sixties; he was a Black guy around my age, Steven.

I asked if they were planning on voting. Steven was affirmative, but she declined to say. I asked Steven which party he was advocating.

"I like Trump," Steven said. "He knows how to make a gathering in a small little town like you wouldn't believe it."

"Nuh-uh," she said. "He has the country so divided."

"There wouldn't be no prisons if we were in uniform," said Steven.

"I have eight brothers and they were all in the military, and all of them are mentally gone," she responded. "I think we should focus on America more than other countries. We're at war with each other."

"Are you a Democrat?"

She inhaled deeply. "I'm going to be honest. I'm one of the people who has a felony. When you have a felony, you have to go through procedures in order to get your voter's rights back. I can't even complain about what's going on, because I don't have my say so in it. But I'm going to get it back."

Out of forty-five industrialized countries sampled, the United States was one of four that stripped felons of their voting rights. This woman wanted to participate in our democracy but was prevented from doing so because of her past. I thought of how American culture often boxed people into old identities, old decisions, old mistakes, without allowing them to grow from them or change. Politicians were punished for evolving on issues and this sometimes cost them elected offices. People who knew the value of evolving and changing, those with past felonies, were barred from even participating in the democratic process to begin with.

I walked down to the docks towards the Bicentennial Observation Tower, a 187-foot structure at the end of the dock. I looked out over the churning waters under iron skies. Nestled in the harbor was the Victorian Princess, a fondant-white cruise ship with a bright red paddlewheel. Next to the ship, I noticed a bearded man in a cap casting a fishing line into the lake. He looked like an Erie local; I asked for an interview.

"I'm trying to enjoy some time off, I work 50 hours roofing. I may not be the most well-spoken guy around, but..." he said, adjusting his cap and revealing a word I hadn't seen before.

"I notice your hat says 'deplorable,'" I said. "What did you feel when Hillary coined the term 'deplorable'?"

"At first I thought 'how could she say that'?" he said, casting his line out. "Then I just took it on as a badge of honor. To them we have no common sense, no education. We're just buck-toothed hillbillies with our Bibles and our guns. The media... they don't talk about the way we really are."

"Do you think our country will ever come together?"

He started reeling in. "I don't think we're gonna have peace until the Prince of Peace shows up, and even then for a thousand years he has to rule with a rod of iron. Until after the reign of Christ, we won't have any peace."

A seagull screeched over Lake Erie.

"So what are you fishing for?"

"Yellow perch. The tastiest fish in the world. Beautiful too."

"Well, best of luck," I said.

I walked away down the dock. I sincerely hoped it wouldn't take Christ's iron rod to bring this country together.

I spent election night in Swarthmore (population 6,257) for the election night party of a Democratic congressional candidate, Mary Gay Scanlon. I sampled lukewarm macaroni bites in the Swarthmore Inn ballroom and watched the results roll in. The Pennsylvania Congressional races were called early—Scanlon won. She came out onto the stage with her family, all smiles and waves, and made a speech. "I know this honor comes with great responsibility as we turn the page on this chapter of our politics. You've entrusted me to work with a new Congress, one that looks a bit different than the ones that came before it." That evening, Pennsylvania elected four new Democratic women to the House of Representatives and re-elected their Democratic governor two years after voting for Donald Trump. Depending on which side you were on, the change in party control in Congress proved that democracy still had a pulse.

One of the more bizarre moments of my travels came during my visit to Philadelphia (population 1.579 million). I stayed with a friend who was in town directing a show. Seonjae, a Korean theatre director and friend from college, and I strolled through Philly's Chinatown. She was the first person with whom I discussed my decision to go to the Trump rally in-person, and Seonjae helped me put my mind at ease as I scrolled through a barrage of new Instagram messages: nothing was wrong with collecting stories.

On Instagram, I noticed a new message from someone I didn't know that started with "love your project." Always a sucker for a bit of positive affirmation, I opened the message from "Scott."

"Love your project. I'm a tour guide at a local historic cemetery, Laurel Hill. Would love to offer you a free tour."

Free things hadn't presented themselves to me too often on this trip, so I threw caution to the wind and made plans to meet Scott at the cemetery after confirming it was indeed a legit tour. On the cab ride over, I got a message from Scott. "Oh, by the way, have you ever been hypnotized before?"

The line between a good opportunity and a red flag was getting thinner and thinner. I told Scott I had, in fact, never been hypnotized. When I arrived at the gorgeous cemetery overlooking autumn bluffs above the river and met Scott, there was no mention of hypnotism.

I was both taken aback and put at ease to discover that Scott was around my age. I found his tour fascinating. The graves were a mixture of headstones, beautiful mausoleums, and moss-covered obelisks. The cemetery, founded in 1836, had free events for people of all ages: concerts, plays, tours, and movie nights.

"We have garden party receptions here," Scott said, motioning to a section of the cemetery. "It might sound sacrilegious to some, but this ancient Egyptian-style tomb right here was actually the bar for one of our events."

"Do you feel when people come here, they get to check in with their mortality?"

"Absolutely," Scott said. "One of my fellow tour guides actually bought a plot here. She is cognizant of death, but it's her connections in life that makes her want to be here. Gives her a feeling of continuity. It's not just death, and that's it," he paused. "Well, maybe it is. But even after death, even if it's death and then nothing. Life may be over for one person, but it's not the death of all stories, you know?"

At the end of the hour-long tour, the cemetery was closing down. I had to ask about the hypnotism.

"Oh, well..." Scott said, looking embarrassed. "I'm sort of an amateur hypnotist."

This was definitely not one of the states of mind I was expecting to encounter.

"Do you... want to try it?" he asked tentatively.

Again, the line between a good story and a risk. "Sure. I'll try."

"Do you want to go somewhere, or...?"

This should've been a red flag, but I said, "no, here is fine."

We proceeded to sit on a bench next to a grave. Scott began counting down, telling me to visualize walking down a dark staircase. I was trembling with cold—the sun was starting to set—but I tried my best to stay open-minded. I had once been called onstage for "Hypnosis Improv" at the Edinburgh Fringe Festival. I had been "hypnotized" to perform improv with members of the cast of "Whose Line is it Anyway?" Though I was not even a little hypnotized, the strong power of the audience and the desire to not break the magic had, in some ways, compelled me to do what was asked of me as if I was. Afterwards, I pretended I hadn't remembered a thing about the ridiculous improv choices I had made—I had simply "blacked out"—and people seemed to believe me. When Scott suddenly snapped and said "SLEEP!" I felt my body drop. I didn't want to ruin the illusion.

He continued this pattern of snapping me in and out of my "conscious mind" and "unconscious mind" and deliberately wanted to know which mind he was addressing.

"Will Ryan's conscious mind remember this conversation?" he asked intently.

Wow, I was glad I was not actually hypnotized. Playing along, I tried to answer the way I assumed he wanted me to. "I… no. He won't."

A few more snaps later, Scott must've been satisfied with how he had gotten me between my two states of being. Scott asked my unconscious mind, "what did Ryan think when he was coming here today?"

"A little nervous," I said, now realizing this was the understatement of the century.

"What did he think of me when he met me?"

Oh, no.

"Interesting," I said, both my conscious and unconscious minds racing to come up with non-sexual adjectives. "Nice."

"Did he find me attractive?"

And suddenly, just like that, I broke out of my hypnotism, citing my need to go to the bathroom.

Scott, flustered, led me to the gate of the cemetery. I called an Uber, wondering how I could possibly pass the next six minutes.

We got to the exit and Scott jiggled the handle of the gate. I was horrified to discover it was locked.

I reached into my pocket and clicked my pen's point into the ready position. If he had a knife, I was going to pen him in the neck like Rachel McAdams in *Red Eye*. I could tell he was worried because he suddenly shouted, "SLEEP."

I pretended to crumple. I didn't want to anger this man who allowed us to get locked in a cemetery.

Scott sounded extremely upset. "Um… can you tell Ryan's consciousness… can you tell his consciousness not to worry? Or let him know that this was always the plan?"

I used my "sleeping" state to suss out my options. *I could jump the fence, I think.* I was not going to die here. I was thinking of all the mausoleums Scott had shown me, all the places to hide my body that only he knew. I couldn't die yet—I was only nine states in, dammit!

Finally, snapping into my conscious mind, I suggested jumping the ten-foot fence. He agreed, and I climbed up with relative ease. I noticed Scott was struggling. My Uber would be here soon… did I help this person who had attempted to have his way with me out of the graveyard, or did I leave him there for the night for his sins?

I chose mercy and helped the poor struggling hypnotist down from the wall. I caught my Uber and escaped my first sinister brush with danger. It would, due to my trusting nature, not be my last.

The rolling hills of West Virginia gave me a foggy welcome as I drove towards a town with a democracy in crisis. My impression of West Virginia before visiting was of a state with a devotion to coal mining. Hillary Clinton had not won a single county in the 2016 West Virginia primary after declaring "we're going to put a lot of coal miners and coal companies out of business" during a CNN town hall. (The remainder of the quote, "and we're going to make it clear that we don't want to forget those people," didn't stick.) However, I arrived and found a town energized by a common enemy: a new "job-creating" factory in the community.

I was visiting Jefferson County. It was clear when I drove into Shepherdstown (population 1,802) that a movement was afoot. All across the county I saw homemade red signs that read "TOXIC ROCKWOOL" or "STOP ROCKWOOL" in yards and outside of businesses. I was meeting with Tony, a former coal mine safety advisor who was going to be driving me around the area. He was a retired man with a palpable sense of passion for community organizing and progressive politics. Our scheduled one-hour tour ended up lasting five.

"Okay, so what is Rockwool?"

Tony clapped his hands together. "You know the name already!"

"I only saw about 70 signs on the way in."

Tony laughed. "Rockwool makes mineral wool. Basically, they take rocks and melt them into lava and make insulation. The end product is arguably very good for creating energy-efficient buildings, but the process with which they make it is dirty, extremely unhealthy. And Rockwool will have two 210-foot smokestacks putting out formaldehyde into the environment as well as into the wastewater stream. We have an incredibly beautiful historic community here in Jefferson County, and this business just absolutely does not fit in. So we've had over 12,000 people come together over the past few months to protest Rockwool. We've been organizing: we've had a series of meetings, we've done research, we've written letters, we have lawsuits to fight this heavily polluting industry. They bought the property, they put in sewers, but they cannot put up the building until they get approval from the city."

Tony wanted me to see what was at risk before showing me the site of Rockwool. Driving me to Harper's Ferry (population 281), he parked at the top of a hill and took me on a rocky hike towards a peak overlooking a river that forked between West Virginia, Maryland, and Virginia.

"The site they're building Rockwool on, it's a sinkhole," he said, lips pursed. "They did tests to see how long it would take for runoff to make it to the river here. How long do you think?"

I had no idea. "Five years?"

Tony laughed humorlessly. "Two weeks."

We stood, overlooking the mountains, watching two hikers crossing the bridge from West Virginia to Maryland. "People come here to hike: imagine what they'll think seeing two giant smokestacks over the horizon." He pointed west. "There's a horse track over there, another source of our tourism. Do you know how polluted air affects horses?"

I could guess. "Not good?"

"*Not good!*" repeated Tony, exhaling as we hiked back towards the car. "Oh, see that rock over there? Thomas Jefferson sat there."

As we drove towards the site, we passed farmland. A lone train car sat behind the fence; the side of the train car displayed a large sign with a hand-painted sheep: "SPINNING ROCK INTO WOOL? BAAAA!" Tony explained how a bipartisan movement had sparked because of Rockwool, resulting in Rockwool supporters being voted off the city council just that week during the midterm elections.

"What percentage of the population would you say is against this?"

"We now know that it's 80/20 against Rockwool, according to a pro-business conservative who lost the election. He said 'anyone who doesn't think this election is about Rockwool hasn't been listening.'"

"So what does winning look like?"

"It will have to happen in the courts. There is little will on the state level to stop this. Governor Justice is a supporter. If we can stop the sewer from going in, cut off the water supply, there's a chance. I don't know if we can stop the gas, but if we can cut off the heart, the utilities, you can stop the business. There's some hope in the political arena, but we think our hope is at the legal level."

I wondered why the state government wasn't heeding the hundreds of red signs across the region. "How many jobs is this supposed to create? Thousands?"

Tony laughed long and hard. "They're only obligated to create 120 jobs to get the tax breaks."

"What? That's *it*?"

"That's it."

"So there's no real economic benefit?"

"Oh, quite the opposite," Tony said. "It will have a deleterious effect on a number of industries, tourism, our orchards, our active horse track, horse owners, and beekeepers. You don't want 210-foot smokestacks spewing phenols and other harmful things into the air and water. And we know that these heavy industries have a tremendously negative effect on children, on the elderly, anyone with a compromised immune system, and they're putting it across the street from an *elementary school* for goodness sake."

"*What?*"

Tony looked stunned. "Didn't I mention that?"

I shook my head.

"Let me show you."

Tony drove me on a country road to an elementary school across from an empty field.

"So where's the factory going to be then?" I asked, looking into the distance.

Tony pointed at the empty field directly across the street from the school. I had overlooked the deep pits dug into the ground, and as we rounded a corner, I could see the construction vehicles waiting to further develop the insulation factory. The school was going to be less than a hundred yards from those smokestacks.

"And behind the school is the poorest neighborhood in Jefferson County, Fox Glenn."

We drove around Fox Glenn. It was a neighborhood of trailers and concrete homes, some with translucent plastic rather than glass in the windows. Tricycles littered the yards. A man waved at us from a lawn chair. I heard a family chatting animatedly in Spanish as we drove past. It was the only neighborhood where there wasn't a single anti-Rockwool sign.

"Are some actually in support of the factory?"

"Of course not. They were paid off," Tony said.

We drove back and parked on the edge of the Rockwool lot. We sat in the car and watched as contractors and builders carried on with their duty of spreading "economic opportunity" to a town that wanted nothing to do with it.

"So what happens if you lose? What happens if the factory gets built?"

Tony thought for a second, gazing out at an excavator. "We've come together in a way I've never seen in the 31 years I've been here. We have an incredible community, don't get me wrong, but we have the same political divisions as other places. This support against Rockwool cuts across every political line, every economic strata. I believe it's going to make our community that much stronger. People should decide what their community looks like. Not every industry is a good one and not every industry fits within every community."

A truck from the site was driving in our direction. Tony put his car in reverse. "But we've also discovered what we're capable of as a community," Tony said, taking a last look at the site, "and the discovery of that power is worth something."

I drove away from West Virginia with a feeling of certainty. The common oppressor of the people wasn't those from the opposing parties. Shepherdstown's plea for self-determination was trumped by the wishes of Rockwool's shareholders. Ironically, it took big business's lack of regard for the community to rally around a common enemy. The left versus right culture war was all a distraction. The corporate media, too, profited off our outrage, our distrust. But at the end of the day, the people of Jefferson County were able to cut through the noise to see what united them all: their town, their air, their water, their kids, their community.

The role of arts in the community was a major theme from both Kentucky and Indiana. In Louisville (population 620,118), I visited The Actors Theatre, a world-class regional theatre in the Bluegrass State. The Actors Theatre was home to the annual Humana New Play Festival, which drew coastal dwellers to a "flyover" state, both as audience members, artists, and apprentices as part of a nine-month program for recent college grads. The theatre found a way to balance more daring, political work with Humana Festival, alongside shows that catered to the community, like annual productions of *A Christmas Carol* and *Dracula*. I wondered how the model created by Actors Theatre, which hired local actors and produced local work as well, could be replicated to give more regional diversity in the arts and the media. With the advent of services like Netflix, Hulu, and Amazon, I was wondering if the monikers of "Hollywood elites" and "New York liberal media" would become obsolete if media actually came from a diversity of regional perspectives. If storytelling shaped the zeitgeist, wasn't it in democracy's best interest to redistribute the storytelling industry throughout the country, rather than the hubs of L.A. and New York? I believed that this would both empower communities and allow people all over the United States to understand a diversity of experiences in the country according to the people who lived there, rather than Hollywood writers. This decentralization of the entertainment industry to increase empathy and support the community was a big job, but luckily I found someone who was trying.

In Indianapolis (population 872,680), I visited the Harrison Center for the Arts, "a community-based, nonprofit arts organization that seeks to be a catalyst for renewal in the city." The founder, Joanna Beatty Taft, was an energetic woman who exuded an easy confidence as she gave me a tour of the premises and outlined how since its founding in 2001, what started as an arts organization to keep artists from abandoning the city became a vessel for community development.

A Washington D.C. native, Joanna was cognizant of the fact that if she had stayed in a city oversaturated with talent, she would not have been able to accomplish half of what she had in Indianapolis, fighting through a crowd of do-gooders. "The lack of red tape doesn't hurt either," admitted Joanna as she walked me through the studios of painters, printmakers, and sculptors. In a wide showroom, portraits of joyful-looking African American seniors were painted in bright colors.

"Those are commissioned portraits of our Great-triarchs," she said, explaining that it had been a priority to give the neighborhood a sense of ownership over the center. "At their hearts, all neighbors want to be known and loved. When you move into a neighborhood and ignore the history, people don't understand how hurtful that is. It's about knowing and loving that story and choosing to be a part of that story. And so we're building community through the arts."

I asked Joanna what it was about the arts specifically that was so impactful.

"I think all people tend to judge. And I think when I meet people, I judge. Art has taught me to listen, to learn, before I decide. I love the arts, because I think it works on your heart."

Joanna told me about the Harrison Center's neighborhood outreach through an interactive festival called a Pre-Enactment. Instead of recreating the way the community used to be, they started a street festival which asked the neighborhood to imagine the most aspirational version of what they wanted their community to look like. All of the neighbors set up booths, played live music, and created a version of the neighborhood that wasn't separated by class or racial barriers. Two months before the Pre-Enactment, three new gentrifying restaurants came into the neighborhood. "And so I went to those businesses, those new businesses, and I asked, 'How are you going to change your business practices to support the neighborhood?' They looked at me like I was crazy," Joanna said as she walked me into the newest wing of the Center, a refurbished church. *"But,* all three businesses came back to me within a month and said, 'we're going to pay a living wage, we're going to hire locally, we're going to support the community.' They ended up getting involved with the Pre-Enactment, and with that in their social muscle memory, these businesses have a sense of what's at stake in the community."

Joanna explained how she tried to live out these community-building principles in her daily life as well. "When we first moved here, we had a front porch, but one of the first things we did when we moved in was put up a privacy fence, because that's what you do in D.C.," she said. "But now, I 'porch' every Sunday afternoon with my neighbors. The Great-triachs come spend time on my porch. We have all these traditions because we've been doing it so long. It's something that didn't happen in D.C., which was more of a private backyard place. So I love that Indianapolis has brought me opportunity, it's brought me access, and it also has the amenities of a city, but it feels like a small town. And I think in our hearts, we all want to live in a small town."

This comment hit me like a gong. I *did* want to live in a small town. The thing that had been unfulfilling to me being involved in the arts in Los Angeles and New York had been the fact that it was primarily a business. To me, the Harrison Center was the best of America. A socially-minded arts organization, the Harrison Center was promoting the arts as a set of values, a lifestyle. The arts are a method to celebrate the places we live, and to make our narratives feel seen, valued, and shared. Kentucky and Indiana left me puzzling about the connection between arts, community, storytelling, and democracy.

. . .

As a kid, when another friend moved away from Rockford or when New American Theatre closed, I convinced myself that if we had stayed in Madison, it all would've been different. Before I lived in Rockford, I lived in Madison, the capital of Wisconsin. It was an idyllic place for a childhood, consistently ranked in the top places to live with plenty of parks and playgrounds, the free Henry Vilas Zoo on the lake downtown, good public schools, and a thriving arts scene through the Madison Civic Center. When I was eight, my parents yanked me from my Madison school and my little community, moving me from one of the most ideal cities to one of the statistical worst. It was a move that took years to fully accept: I still remember the feeling of youthful displacement and the tinges of resentment it brought. If a demagogue had come along and played upon my eight-year-old frustrations, perhaps they would've found a receptive audience.

I backtracked towards Wisconsin to spend the Thanksgiving holidays with my family. Since Madison was one of those blueberries floating in tomato soup (a liberal city in reddish Wisconsin), I decided to forgo my nostalgia. Instead, I arrived in Racine (population 78,860) for Thanksgiving at my Aunt Kim and Uncle Kevin's house. I've been blessed with a tight, close-knit family—our extended family gatherings are full of guffawing, card-playing, and incessant teasing. As we piled stuffing on our plates, this sense of belonging felt particularly poignant after what I had witnessed over the past month. The security I felt in my family and my social safety net was part of what gave me the courage to venture out. When all else failed, I had a place to belong. On de Tocqueville's visit, he remarked that Americans "of all ages, all stations in life, and all types of dispositions are forever forming associations." Here, with my family, I felt that connection.

The next day, Aunt Kim reminded me of our obligation to spread that social capital. Waking both my cousin Annie and me early, she drove us downtown to the Racine Hospitality Center, which—in their own words—aims "to provide hospitality without agenda to those in need or underserved in Racine: the homeless, near homeless, and mentally ill." We arrived at a large church gymnasium and helped set up both a hot and cold buffet. Soon, a line began to form around the gymnasium. People of all ages and ethnicities were queued up for food, but the spirit inside mirrored the Thanksgiving I had just come from. Older Black men in veteran's hats slapped guffawing young white guys with dreads on the back as Aunt Kim, Annie, and I snapped hair nets on our heads and began to dish out the food.

As people approached, I was surprised to see many whom, at first glance, I wouldn't have pegged as needing these services. A meek older woman approached me, dressed like a typical kindergarten teacher. Another man had put on his best blazer. Every single person said thank you.

The Hospitality Center was run by Carl Fields, a tall Black man with a broad smile and wonkish charm. After spending 17 years in a maximum security prison, Carl is now a Racine community organizer. After the meal, Carl talked candidly about how at the age of 18, grieving the death of his mother, he had fired at a police officer during a drug raid. The prison system, which he described as "built to grind you up and spit you out as an individual," was only made worse by how he fared when he reentered the community.

"As an ex-incarcerated person, having seen the other side, I've seen the twisted narratives and I've seen the inaccuracies that are allowed to continue and the millions of dollars that we throw at those inaccuracies," said Carl. "Potential employers weren't willing to get over that social hump, because it's socially acceptable to discriminate against people who've been incarcerated." Carl talked about how the easiest way to stay financially flush would have been to relapse into activities that had landed him in jail in the first place, but he was privileged enough to have support and couches to crash on during his search for employment.

Carl talked about his decision to come back to the Hospitality Center to work with the shelter. As a former homeless child, he wanted to give back to people who were going through struggles that were sometimes invisible and give them a place for support. Carl was simultaneously one of the gentlest and sharpest people I had met on the trip. The unwillingness of some members of society to see Carl as more than his incarceration robbed them of the opportunity to see the dynamic, passionate person he had become.

I left my family reluctantly and traveled north to Appleton (population 72,623), a riverfront town that's home to most of my family's alma mater: Lawrence University. I had an interview with Mayor Tim Hanna, one of the longest-serving mayors in the country, who took office in 1996. Appleton is an objectively thriving town, constantly topping lists of the best places to live in the country. Hanna, a bespectacled Republican with a friendly face, revealed one of the town government's secrets to a happy community: an active City Hall Facebook page.

When Hanna told me this, I was perplexed. I had begun diagnosing social media as one of the primary disruptors of democratic cohesion, yet the popular mayor went on to explain how with their weekly "What's Your Question Wednesday" the community had an opportunity to directly ask questions to their city government and get a response. Question topics varied from speed bumps to road closures to "why do people think *Attack of the Clones* is good?" (Appleton City Hall replied, "probably just because of the *Star Wars* in front of it.") The response to this question was the only major controversy I saw in the over 305 comments from the most recent post. Maybe it was something about the inherent Wisconsin decency, but it seemed like this community could find a way to have their voices heard and hold their government accountable without getting angry or polarized.

I sped up to Green Bay (population 105,116) and had a second Thanksgiving with some friends from college, culminating in seeing one of their cousins in a very amusing high school production of *Mamma Mia!* (you haven't experienced the true meaning of "The Winner Takes it All" until you've heard it belted out by a high school junior). I stayed that night with my friends, a married couple with an adorable dog. Perhaps due to my recent departure from my family, I felt a pang of loneliness. Experiencing this trip on my own was exhilarating, and I was almost never without company. But after all of the greetings and goodbyes, what I really wanted was someone in Belinda's passenger seat to experience the journey with.

The next day, I decided to drive further north, noticing flurries as I passed into the industrial lakefront town of Marinette (population 10,607). I was headed into Michigan's Upper Peninsula, which I felt was given less attention than the mainland mitten of Michigan. The problem was that the little flurries, so light and atmospheric in Wisconsin, were now coming down the size of corn flakes. Driving on the one-lane road, it became obvious that if I wanted to talk to a local, I'd better hurry. I stepped into the White Tail Restaurant & Motel in Brevort (population 976) as the storm was raging. Inside, there were only a few customers.

"I'll be right with you, hon," a young waitress in an orange t-shirt said, passing me with a tray of dishes.

I sat down and ordered the special: a whitefish sandwich. As the waitress bussed the table, I asked if I could interview her.

She came over five minutes later with a tray of silverware and napkins to roll. I started asking her what life was like in the U.P.

"It's tough livin' up here, I'll be honest," she said, polishing a fork and tossing it into the basket. "Employment is hard. Just heading up US-2, a lot of businesses are closed for the winter and they make it so difficult to get your unemployment."

"How would you describe the culture politically? Do people lean one way or another?"

She tossed another napkin full of silverware into the basket.

"That's a touchy one. Because it's so hard living up here, people want to see change, and the right change. There was a gentleman who came in here last summer talking about Trump. He hates Trump. I love Trump, I'm absolutely loving what he's doing for our country. And he asked me, and I told him. He started yelling, it was almost a full blown argument."

"While you were working?"

"Yeah. So I had to back down."

She explained how a lot of people, like this particular patron, just come to the U.P. for the summer, leaving the locals to struggle through long winters when work was scarce. I sensed that there was a slight resentment towards those who visited for the beautiful summer months and then left the community to fend for itself when the weather and economy got rough.

Having lived in both worlds, I felt the pain of the people in the Rust Belt, but I also had heard the misconceptions from those who had never visited. Coastal dwellers, especially after 2016, assumed these people were ignorant and had a lack of interest in the places outside of their own backyards. It was a string of misunderstandings. Rust Belt denizens assumed others looked down on them. I've encountered this: after the 2016 election, a lifelong New Yorker told me that Midwesterners are racists, before I gently reminded her that I was from the Midwest. If this friend from the Upper West Side could sit down at the cafe in Brevort and talk to Marie, perhaps over a couple of drinks they would find that they really wanted the same things.

I quickly paid my bill and tipped Marie, and Belinda skidded towards the bridge that would take me to the mainland. We approached it, a green iron giant with cables vaulting across the lake. Belinda drove along the metal slats below, making a dissonant, rumbling sound like the worst Gregorian chant you've ever heard. The storm raged as I traversed above the lake, and I felt a sense of wonder.

I arrived at my next stop in East Lansing. I was meeting with a teacher named Jeff Crowley at a local diner. Jeff was a tall, animated theatre instructor and self-described "talent developer" from the local public school. After the eyebrow-raising antics of the life-preserver and flipper-filled production of *Mamma Mia!* in Green Bay, I was starting to question the "why" of high school theatre. This was a question shared by Jeff.

Jeff told me how at his school, he had developed a new way of making theatre: the students write their own sketch show lampooning their school, their community, and national politics. "It's important, the concept of laughing at oneself to fully understand who you are," he explained. Through researching issues at the local, state, national, and global level and trying to find the humor, students have to show a mastery of the issues but also need to be objective about their own opinions to be truly funny.

"So it actually becomes a mix between performing arts and civics?"

"Oh, yeah. Everything should be about civics," Jeff said, putting jam on his toast.

For the first time on my journey, I was trying to outrun the weather by driving south. As I drove, I thought of something that had been bothering me. In the 2016 election, 107,000 voters in Michigan, Pennsylvania, and Wisconsin changed the course of history. Hillary won the popular vote by nearly three million. These states had gone for Trump by margins of 68,235 votes, 27,257 votes, and 11,837 votes respectively. 107,000 people. 0.09% of the electorate. In contrast, in 2016, "1,920,718 Americans graduated with a bachelor's degree." My own college, Northwestern University, sent 36.4% of its graduates to Chicago, followed by New York and San Francisco. Even if someone I knew hadn't moved to California or New York, the vast majority had moved to cities in blue states, like Denver, Portland, or Seattle. If 10% of overwhelmingly progressive college graduates who voted Democratic had moved to Wisconsin, Pennsylvania, or Michigan, we might be living in a very different political reality.

But it was also about more than the Electoral College. Why did the best educated people flock to the largest, most competitive, "best" cities? According to a study by the Wall Street Journal, "only 62 institutions in our database see more than half of their alumni move to smaller metropolitan and rural areas." The top 5 places that college students went, according to the study, were New York, Washington D.C., Los Angeles, Chicago, and San Francisco. If the educated elites were choosing en masse not to participate in the heartland, where so many places were hungry for talent, perhaps there was truth to the optics that liberals didn't care about anyone outside of the blue states.

A moment of clarity hit me like a sunbeam across Belinda's windshield. Was there not a different kind of inequality seeping into the fabric of our democracy, a regional inequality? We needed more than a change of party in the White House or Congress: we needed a return to the equality of our democracy that Tocqueville admired. Democracy couldn't function if we saw some regions as more important, some states as more valuable, and some perspectives as more legitimate, but maybe embracing the diverse states of mind in our country started with embracing our own community. I'd seen so many Americans get off social media and use their talents—organizing, protesting, volunteering, teaching, painting, debating, or just listening—to make their communities more cohesive and inclusive. If we could foster that small-town feeling of belonging, being listened to, and having a purpose in the community, perhaps we could begin to cool down the rhetoric that had sent our democracy into a fever. From what I had seen, it didn't just seem good for democracy. It seemed to be a roadmap to fulfillment.

I drove south, thinking about the future.

THE SOUTH ATLANTIC STATES

Colin Woodward explains that the United States comprises of eleven distinct regions in his book *American Nations: A History of the Eleven Rival Regional Cultures of North America*. These regions, shaped by colonial settlements, have their own cultures and belief systems based on a shared history. As a Northerner, I wanted to be cognizant of my lack of context regarding Southern identity and to ensure I didn't irresponsibly lump them together. Grouping Maryland, a state in a region Woodward defined as "Tidewater" (described as "conservative; [with] respect for authority and tradition, not equality or political participation") which included Delaware, Maryland, and parts of Virginia and North Carolina in with other Southern states didn't sit right with me at first. However, I discovered that was, in fact, exactly how the Census of the United States categorized them: census data grouped Delaware and Maryland in with the Southern states like South Carolina, Georgia, and Florida in a region called "The South Atlantic States." These were states associated with the original 13 Colonies, and each was below the Mason-Dixon line, the line used to separate Northern free states and Southern slave states—every state I was about to visit being one of latter. It didn't feel like it as I drove across the Midwest to my first stop in Delaware, but apparently I was in the South.

As I entered Delaware, I luckily now had a travel companion. Julia was one of my oldest friends from college. We had spent a hilarious three months in a professional production of *A Christmas Carol* in the Wisconsin Dells at a theatre where our checks regularly bounced and we lived in housing appropriately called "the gulag." Picking her up at the bus station, I spotted her red hair and wry smile and immediately felt a rush of joy. Julia was someone who was always game for a journey and brought a sense of mischief to the ride.

We stopped for pancakes at Bob Evans, a diner chain. Julia is the type of friend who will always be in your corner when it matters but won't hesitate to tell you the things you need to know. On today's menu was "your sunglasses are crooked."

We were staying with Jim, a warm former pastor. We arrived at his house on the outskirts of Smyrna (population 10,023) where Jim and his wife welcomed us. Since retiring, Jim had poured his entire being into writing plays and organizing the community for a new library.

"It's too small, there aren't enough computers, and there's no room for books," Jim said with a pastor's fire, towering over us in his kitchen. "Smyrna needs a new library if we want to be an attractive place for new families." He told us how the library committee he sat on, a group of about twenty, had been working on this project for twelve years.

Julia and I had agreed a few weeks in advance to participate in a fundraiser for the Friends of the Duck Creek Regional Library organization. Julia and I were going to read children's books to the attendees, which at the time we assumed would be children, so Jim drove us to see the library in question and to pick out some reading material. We pulled up to a grand brick building in the heart of downtown.

Jim's being a little melodramatic? Julia's look seemed to say to me as we walked up to the building.

"So this is the library that needs updating, Jim?" I asked, gesturing to the grand old building.

"Oh! Oh, no. This is the Smyrna Opera House," Jim said matter-of-factly as we walked around the perimeter.

"Where's the library?" I asked.

We rounded a corner. A tiny sign jutted out from the annex of the building, advertising the "Duck Creek Library." It was indeed as Jim said. Cramped as a trailer, we entered the tiny library to find a room six shelves long and filled with old computers and elderly librarians. As soon as they saw Julia and me, the librarians grinned with excitement.

"They're here!" they cried, positively dancing up to us. We looked at Jim, confused.

Jim reached down behind the librarian's desk and pulled out a newspaper. "I may have let the local paper know you were coming…"

We looked down to find Julia's face and my face smoldering from the entertainment page of *The Smyrna/Clayton Sun Times*.

"How did you find our headshots?" she asked, guffawing at our feature.

Jim shrugged. "Facebook."

The fundraiser was the next day, so that afternoon, Julia and I decided to drive down to the capital city of Dover (population 37,523). Raindrops began to hit Belinda's windshield, and by the time we arrived we were in an all-out thunderstorm. Rather than walking around the quaint, cobblestoned downtown, we ended up opting for an inside activity. We toured the Delaware capitol building, which was virtually empty. We strolled in and out of the ornate legislative chambers and chatted with a security guard, as we were the only visitors there.

Walking back to our car under an umbrella, we passed a

modern brick building radiating a warm glow in the gloom. Julia nudged me.

"It's a library."

Inside, the place was mercifully dry, crowded with people, from moms reading with their kids to bedraggled folks visibly happy to have a place out of the rain. We found the head librarian, Karen, a soft-spoken, short-haired woman, and told her we had just come from Smyrna.

"I know very well the struggle Duck Creek is going through. It took twenty years to build this library, and I don't mean the construction," she told us in her office. "I think how libraries function in communities has changed. They are no longer the 'beloved book institutions' that they were for hundreds of years. Because we do things now like serve marginalized communities. And we welcome everyone into our building. And not everybody likes that. So it can be very controversial."

"And by everyone, you mean…?"

"There's a big population of homeless people in Dover. They don't come here for services. What they want is a place to sit. Not in the rain, not in the snow. They need a place to *be*. Whether or not the library is the most appropriate community place for that, I'm not sure. But there aren't any other alternatives for them." She pointed to a placid man in a polo shirt, reading a hardcover novel next to the rainy windowpane. "He comes and reads all day long. He gets a book in the morning, reads, and at the end of the day puts the books back. Every day."

There was a rumble of thunder.

She sighed. "Some of our community won't come here because we let the homeless use our building. But that's their choice. They have other places they can go, if they're lucky enough to have those resources. But not everybody is." As Karen described, libraries were now lifting more responsibility than just providing education and activities. They were also taking on the burden of other local issues that didn't have funding and solutions.

The next morning, Julia and I arrived at the backroom of a church to headline the brunch fundraiser. We watched as, instead of the children we were expecting, 30 adult women showed up. Julia and I read *The Rainbow Fish* and *The Snowy Day* to the women in their 70s. To appease the unexpectedly mature audience, Julia and I finished off the performance by reading the balcony scene from *Romeo and Juliet*. A woman in the audience cheered. I saw Julia's lips twitch into a small, incredulous smile.

After polite applause, former Mayor Joanne Masten gave a rousing speech about what the library would do for the community. As I stood and listened, I felt a nudge.

A heavily-jeweled woman with a walker peered up at me.

"That reading, the Shakespeare one," she said, nodding at Julia, "that was sexy as hell."

"Oh! Thank you so much," I said, over Joanne's call to action.

"You and Miss Redhead make a cute couple," she said, winking. "But don't you forget what they say about older ladies. We don't tell, we don't swell, and we're always grateful as hell!"

De Tocqueville did not have a quote that was applicable to this situation.

There was something about Maryland and Delaware that had a bit of sameness to me. As we crossed the river into Baltimore, Julia and I laughed about my experience after going to the rally. It suddenly felt like a long time away.

"The corporate media, big finance. Those are who we should be going after. Not some mom of four from the suburbs of Cleveland."

Julia, as a self-described member of "Hot Girls for Bernie" at the time, was as liberal as they could come, and I was relieved to find she was not mad about me going to a Trump Rally.

"We shouldn't be villainizing the believers in the Trump movement. The real people destroying democracy are those affecting the narrative that causes people to constantly be outraged."

Off of a friend's suggestion, we were heading to the Lexington Market in Baltimore (population 576,498), which is like something frozen in time. It was completely un-yuppified, full of stalls with neon signs advertising "Sipes Poultry," "Lexington Fried Chicken," and "Buffalo Bill's II" gleaming on off-white subway tiles. The butcher shops seemed not to have been updated since the early 1990s, and I saw a few Pepsi advertisements straight out of the '80s. I loved every inch of it.

We made our way past the John W. Faidley raw seafood bar ("Oysters - Clams - Beer") flanked by framed photographs of a blonde woman with a wide smile and crab jewelry holding multiple awards. We made our way toward the neon "Faidley's" sign above an extensive menu.

"What should we get?"

Julia pointed to the most conspicuous menu item. "The Award-Winning Jumbo Lump Crab Cake seems like a good bet."

We paid for our meal and were given what looked like a deep-fried baseball next to a plate of salad. We stood at the counter, examining it. Finally, I took a bite.

If nothing else panned out on this journey, it was worth it for this crab cake.

"Ryan."

I had never tasted a crab cake with such generous portions of crab, the perfect amount of panko. Was there mayonnaise based into the cake itself?

"Ryan."

I opened my eyes. Julia pointed to a woman emerging from behind the counter. Nancy Faidley, the owner and architect of this perfect dish.

I continued to savor the divine sea-orb and finally we approached the smiling woman.

I asked her how she got into the crab cake business.

Nancy laughed. "Well, it all started when my grandfather was here in 1886. It was all fresh seafood back then. This was an outside market. In the 60s, people started saying 'that smells good, that looks good' so we started selling the food. In 1987, I made the best crab cake in Baltimore and that's the jumbo lump crab cake."

"He's familiar," Julia said, glancing at me.

"So these are all my recipes. In 1992 *GQ* magazine named us top dish of the year. I've been on the Food Network, *Bon Appetit*, *The New York Times*… I was number one in *Baltimore Magazine*, but I got a letter that they had to change the category because I kept winning. Now I'm 82 years old and—"

"No way!"

"Yes, I am. I've seen four generations of people who have worked for me." Nancy smiled and looked around her little corner of the market. "It's funny, nobody wants me to renovate this place. They love the authentic Baltimore feel. All kinds of people. All walks of life. I love it. That's what keeps me here. Seeing people."

Even though it felt like Nancy Faidley was the real mayor of Baltimore, I also had the chance to speak to the woman who was the actual mayor of Baltimore… at the time. In my research before my phone interview with Mayor Catherine Pugh, I saw that she had written her own self-published children's books.

"How did you decide to start writing your own books?" I asked from the bedroom of my friend Drew's guest house outside of Baltimore.

"I asked myself 'how do we begin to educate our young people at an early age about eating right?'" said Pugh, sounding pleased. "So I wrote *Healthy Holly: Exercising is Fun*, *Healthy Holly: Fruits are the Colors of the Rainbow*, and three other books."

I didn't think much of it at the time. However, since I left Maryland, Pugh has resigned due to a massive corruption scandal involving—no, really—*Healthy Holly* herself. Allegedly, her typo-ridden educational books had earned her a $800,000 contract with the Maryland Medical System, which, instead of distributing the self-published books to Maryland schoolchildren as intended, stashed them in a warehouse. It was the epitome of a bribe.

I bought a book and read through the first few pages. The character development, dialogue, and punctuation left something to be desired:

Holly's father is bringing her mother home. She had been at the hospital. She was not sick. Holly's mother had a baby. She had a boy. Today Holly will meet her new brother. Holly thought about all the things she will do with her new brother. She will teach him to be healthy. They will play together. They will jump rope Holly and her new brother will ride bikes.

"Hi, Holly. We are home. Come see your new little brother said her mother."

Holly's dad was holding him. "What is his name?" asked Holly.

"His name is Herbie," said her dad.

When Holly saw baby Herbie, she said he is very small.

"When will he be able to exercise?"

"It will be a while before baby Herbie can do all the things you can do," said Holly's father.

Amazon reviews of the *Healthy Holly* series trend towards one star:

"The lack of any characterization or plot or even flow thru suggests this thing was written in one afternoon by an extremely low IQ person."

"Easy to flip through wearing handcuffs, and the print is big enough to read in prison cell lighting."

But one satisfied buyer gave it 5/5: "I bought 50 of these and finally my rooftop deck permit got approved. 10/10 would buy again."

Obviously, Healthy Holly was not democracy (or writing) at its best.

• • •

Julia went back to New York before Virginia, but her companionship made it very clear that I was happier when there was someone
else in the car with me. I was melancholy and alone as I drove
towards Virginia. I spent time in the D.C. suburb of Alexandria
(population 157,613). I was staying in the home of a family friend,
Mary Kendall, who was at the time the Deputy Inspector General
of the Department of the Interior. Mary was a short woman with an
infectious sense of merriment that could turn into intense focus on
a dime. She had recently drawn the ire of the Trump administration
for investigating Ryan Zinke, the Secretary of the Interior. Sitting in
the passenger seat as she drove into her D.C. office, she talked to
me about the changes she had seen in the politicization of the
federal government that prevented work from getting done.

"The culture in D.C. changes," she told me as we drove past the
Potomac. "When I first started during the Reagan administration,
of course I don't have the view I have now, but it just seemed like
Congress worked better with itself, it worked better with the
administration. The administrations had their policies and their
goals, whatever their promises were during campaigns or elections
—but they seemed more willing to work with the opposing party,
people they needed to work with to get their goals accomplished."

The sun was just rising, casting a pinkish hue over the marble of
the Washington obelisk. "Do you have a good sense of who is
aligned with what party in your department?"

"Most of the professional career folks view civil service as
serving for a long time and serving the administration that is in
power at the time. You kind of have to bite your political tongue on
your personal views. And my *personal* view is as long as what they
are doing is legal, they have a right to change policies, whether I
agree with them or not. There's probably three or four people in my
organization who have any inclination to what my political leaning
is because I mask it all the time, so it's a little bit of a dance."

Mary pulled into the parking garage of the Department of the
Interior, a beautiful neoclassical building with an abundance of rich

murals lining the walls. As she went to work, I walked into the city to speak with a White House correspondent (who wished to remain anonymous) about the culture of the press in Washington D.C. and the belief that journalists, like civil servants, must remain fiercely nonpartisan.

"Why do you think the 'fake news media' insult is resonating?" I asked her.

She jabbed at a salad with relish in a small D.C. cafe, seemingly thrilled to have an outlet to vent.

"Simple. Presenting the media as a foil for the Democratic party makes it easy to discount them if you don't like what they're saying."

"And do you think that's valid?"

She stabbed a beet.

"We all need to work harder—if you're covering politics—to make sure that you're not being biased, and work against any perception that you may be biased. I mean, I don't think journalists should vote."

"Wow."

She shrugged. "If you're the referee, you can't play in the game."

As she picked through the bottoms of her salad, I thought of a political climate where a journalist could actually show such candor.

"Do you think some journalists give people a reason to call the media biased?"

"Of course, I see it now. Some people *have* a bias. I had a colleague at my former employer, and we were both covering the White House, and he left the White House because he became so passionate against the administration that he couldn't cover it anymore. He couldn't just be a bystander, he had to be an advocate, and I think that his writing had some bias in it. People always ask me all the time, 'I don't know how you do your job! Don't you get angry?' No. I don't let myself get upset. I don't see myself as the resistance. I'm not the resistance. None of us are supposed to be the resistance. If people can't trust that we're coming into this with a clear head and without an agenda…" she trailed off. "I want people to question what party I'm affiliated with. How I vote. Even my friends will say 'you're too right-leaning, you're too left,' and that's where you want to be. Because at that point it's like you're standing for a fact, for the truth, for an inconvenient truth."

The door to the cafe opened. She looked over her shoulder, then turned back to me.

"I have friends who glorify the Obama administration, and it's like… really? You think it was all great then too? It wasn't. And Trump does a lot of things that are certainly justified, but the *backlash* and the *outcry*. And sometimes he just gets attacked for decorum and style points. His tweets are how he sets the agenda. And we take the bait. He's using us so much." She scraped her knife against the side of her bowl, picking up remaining avocado. "And I don't want to be used."

The terrain started to turn mountainous as I drove further south into Virginia. I visited Monticello, the home of President Thomas Jefferson, a curiosity of a house that put the founding father's idiosyncrasies on display for all visitors. The neoclassical plantation house, designed by Jefferson himself, sat on a peak in the Southwest Mountains. The slave cabins and servants' quarters, however, were intentionally designed to be out of Jefferson's sight. Jefferson was a perfect example of the contradictions within the brilliant but flawed men who founded our country: a slave-owning inventor who spoke of the rights of all men to liberty. The man whom Alexis de Tocqueville deemed "the greatest Democrat whom the democracy of America has yet produced" had no problem contemplating democracy, but his worldview didn't extend to all.

I ended up in the town of Lexington, Virginia (population 7,042). The weather had turned cold—it was Christmastime. The charming downtown was illuminated with wreaths and Christmas lights; the churches and Georgian architecture made the town look like a Currier and Ives illustration of small-town America. There, I joined a group of carolers who were walking to hospice care centers and nursing homes, singing carols. I stood in the back of a group of fifteen kids and their parents singing "Jingle Bell Rock" to an audience that grinned widely and tapped their toes to the music. I shook bells and exchanged smiles with the adults who were watching their kids with such joy. Afterwards, we stood and ate cupcakes and watched the snow flurries outside. I was filled with good feelings; I loved this little town at the center of the state, and I was happy to be among a group that didn't question why I was there; they must've assumed it was just out of the goodness of my heart.

My next stop was North Carolina. I was going to be at High Point University giving a lecture about my journey so far to the honors students at the university, organized by my godmother, Angie, who was one of the Deans of the college. Angie also set up a meeting between me and the University President, Dr. Nido Quebein, with an aim to discuss the problems of higher education in America. I went to the president's office and met with Nido, a dynamic man with a crisp suit and a white shock of hair, and he exuded great energy as he explained to me what he believed the role of higher education was.

"We are a premiere *life skills* institution," he explained, slicing the air with his hands. "A university is not a business, but a safe atmosphere where students feel like they can debate and dialogue and discuss anything without retribution."

"What do you feel the role of education is in modern society?"

He inhaled, as if gearing up for a long speech.

"You go to a university to acquire three things. Number one, the experience of maturation. You go to a campus alongside other people, from varied backgrounds, learning to deal with people with whom you may disagree."

I perked up. This seemed topical.

Quebein continued. "The number two reason is to take you from a horizontal thinker to a vertical thinker, to focus on the why, plus the how. When you train someone, you show them how, when you have an education, you show them *why*. You become a problem solver, a critical thinker. Number three is about commitment. It's about what I will do with this education. We're all given a purpose to make the world a better place. I am enough as a human being, but I will always be thirsty and hungry to keep learning."

Perhaps it was the hunger to keep learning that led me to drive into the Black Mountains during a blizzard the next day. I was going to visit a commune called Earthhaven that I had found online. I had signed up for a tour and called ahead of time because of the inclement weather but received no answer. I drove 40 minutes into the mountains and pulled onto a gravel road that took me to a village of yurts and tiny homes surrounded by thick forest. I parked next to a pen of sheep adjacent to an aluminum barn, and I called out to a woman who was inside.

"Excuse me! I'm here for the tour."

The woman looked at me then looked up at the falling snow. "It was canceled."

"Oh. I didn't know. I didn't get the—"

She shook her head and smiled. "That's Earthhaven for you. It just didn't really go with the flow of the day." She was in her early thirties with a beautiful homemade scarf wrapped around her neck.

"Understandable," I said. "I wanted to interview someone, but maybe I can call?"

She appraised me. "What the heck… come with me. I can find you someone to talk to."

She led me in between wooden houses and large, circular yurts, between garden plots and upturned wheelbarrows, up towards the largest house at the top of a hill. She pulled out a ring of keys and stuck it in the door. "I'm Sara, by the way."

I heard a moaning sound from inside the house. I was suddenly hit with a wave of fear, remembering I was in the middle of the mountains with very little cell reception.

"I'm Ryan," I said, wondering if I should be treating this as another graveyard hypnosis situation.

It was warm inside the house, which was high-ceilinged, lofted, and roughly built. From the corner, I again heard a faint moaning noise.

"Jeanie!" Sara called upstairs. "I brought someone!"

"I'll be right down!" came a woman's voice from upstairs.

Another moan from the corner. I looked at Sara, slightly unnerved.

"This is Jeanie's house. I come once a week to help take care of her mom." Sara gestured towards the corner, where a small cot stood. At first I thought the bed was covered in a pile of sheets, but when they began to move I realized that the cot was occupied by a small, frail old woman, grasping at the blankets and moaning at the ceiling.

"Mom's in a mood today," said a voice behind me. I watched as a woman with long gray hair descended the stairs with a mug in her hand. "Who's this?"

Sara introduced me, explaining what I was there to do. Minutes later, I was sitting in Jeanie's kitchen, a mug of tea in my hand.

"I made that mug, you know," Jeanie said, nodding at it. "I have a pottery studio here."

"So, that brings me to my first and kind of basic question—what exactly do you do here?"

Sara exchanged a smile with Jeanie. "Well, I live at Earthhaven. And I do a lot of different things. I give tours. I sometimes do some caregiving, that's why I'm here at Jeanie's. I have a shift today with Jeanie's mom. I manage and shop for 'group kitchen.' I teach a couple mornings a week in a homeschool supplementation co-op. I make firewood. I'm the vice-president of my neighborhood housing co-op. Like many here, I cobble together a living, a life."

"So how many people live here?"

"Well, that's a bit complicated," Jeanie said. "We had to undergo this legal restructuring process that's been sucking everybody's energy which is finally coming to an end. Instead of everyone being everything, everyone's house, instead of being under one big homeowner's association, we're creating 'neighborhood entities,' so liability can be owned by smaller entities. There are like 90 people who live at Earthhaven now. So in my co-op there are maybe 18."

Sara chimed in, "And I'm in my own house now, and the yurt I used to own is part of it as well."

"So what is so special about your community?"

Jeanie laughed. "A lot has evolved to get us to Earthhaven. It started out with Rosybranch, which was a land-trust community, then people built houses, sold houses, and brought in new people. I counted one time, when I was trying to go to sleep, the number of people that I know, and I came up with 150. And to have that many people that you know is great. Having kids especially, the fact that anyone they meet is somebody they know, you feel pretty good about just letting them free-range. I've heard that's more how things were in the 1950s, they could jump on their bicycles and do whatever, whereas now if you do that, people will call child services on you."

"So is the goal to form some sort of… utopia?" I asked. "Is it that lofty?"

Jeanie laughed again. "I would say that for the founders, the idea was to show another way that things could be, here is an example of something that could work. And amazingly it has worked for this long, 25 years."

Sara jumped in. "The idea is of a living laboratory, the tantric principle of everything is an experiment—we really have an education mission, and that is both to show our successes and show our failures, and I never hear the word utopia."

"I don't *think* people come here for a simpler way of life…" Jeanie said, looking to Sara.

"I did," Sara said laughing. "But in some ways, it is simpler. I feel my life is simpler. I think maybe because everything I'm doing is tangible to my life. I lived in San Diego, and I worked in an office, and I proofread title insurance reports—what does that even *mean*?—and I listen to punk rock on my headphones while I proof-read, and I drive everywhere, and I shop at Target, and I have very little connection to anything I'm doing. I don't see people face to face. So my life is simpler now, because things are tangible now, most of the things have a direct connection to my life."

"Has it made your life better?"

"So much better. I remember one night, we were preparing for a wedding, and we were all singing together, and it was my first experience with *eros*—not necessarily sexual, but like creative energy."

"That makes me think of the funerals," Jeanie added, "the care-taking around them. Grieving together. And not sending them off somewhere, having them stay here. It's really special. Like, of course there's another way to do something. I want to do things that way."

I looked out the window, where I could see four yurts standing amidst the snowflakes. "So there are clearly a lot of people here, and things have to get done. How do you make decisions as a group?"

Sara chimed in, "I think I will say that it is very much encour-aged to deal with conflicts and not let it linger. Because it does impact more than just you, because everyone is so close here. Espe-cially if it's around a decision."

Jeanie nodded. "Something you would've heard on the tour that I really like to point out, is people have this romantic notion when they move here. They think they're moving to a community of like-minded or like-hearted people, and that immediately translates to 'it's going to be easier, we're going to have the same priorities.' And what I really like to make clear is we don't have a guru, we don't have spiritual beliefs, we don't even share a cosmology. We don't come from the same set of values and motivations. So yes, we're totally like-minded, but within the same fifteen core values or priorities, we all rank them differently. So yeah… there's a ton of conflict."

Sara added, "Currently we use a consensus model. For the majority of Earthhaven's life, it's been unanimous consensus or unanimous consensus minus one and right now we're still using a consensus model, and we're still aiming for unanimity, that's the goal, but after a few steps in the process, it comes down to an 85% supermajority. When I got here, this restructuring thing just got started, and at the time there were a couple of blockers. The tyranny of the minority is the phrase I've heard about what it was like then. There was this feeling that we can't get anything done. And a few years into me being here, there was this decision to move to 85%, and there was this feeling of relief, like things were going to finally start getting done."

As I thought of our Congress, struggling to get to a 60-vote threshold on legislative decisions, Jeanie's mom moaned from the corner, and I took it as my cue to leave.

If it weren't for the ice storm, South Carolina would've been perfect. I had plans to begin the trip by meeting with the mayor of Columbia (population 133,273), Stephen Benjamin. Instead, I was there early, holed up in a Baymont Inn on the outskirts of town, evacuated from the storm. I spent the night looking at houses in my hometown. At this point, Rockford seemed like where I was destined to end up.

I drove toward Greenville, my schedule now out of whack. Another ice storm was coming that afternoon, and I tried to bump my meeting with Knox White, the mayor of Greenville but had to delegate it to a phone call the next week instead. His secretary sounded disappointed on the phone, because "there's so much for you to see in Greenville," so I made time to see for myself.

Greenville (population 67,737) was a magical little town, even in the sleet. The main street had plenty of shops, restaurants, and stores with apartments right above them. As I walked down to the waterfalls at the end of the street, I noticed a sign for a gallery. I walked in and met John, a painter who had recently moved from New York back to Greenville. As he showed me art and described what made him fall in love with the town, I cursed the weather for keeping me from spending more time in this town that really should've been a contender for my future home.

As I drove south to Georgia, I knew that besides looking for a place to live, I was looking for something more. Long a disciple of Joseph Campbell, I believed that everyone who ventured outside their homes and undertook some kind of travel underwent a version of the hero's journey. I had hoped that this trip would similarly become a transformational experience that would provide me with much-needed clarity, not just about our democracy, but where I fit into it.

And, of course, I hoped love fit in there somewhere. I was desperately convinced that on the trip I would somehow fall in love with a place, but I was also hoping that this story would have a romance in the plot. Unfortunately, this caused me to read into even casual interactions with a sort of desperate intensity that this could be the spark of a beautiful love story. A romantic at heart, I could infuse the mundane with meaning and easily confuse friendly conversation with something transcendent. Admittedly, I had also occasionally indulged myself in checking out the local culture, through some combination of Tinder and Hinge which made me feel even more lonely when I had to get back on the road.

I had experienced two romantic letdowns the summer before. One was with a Parisian whom I had been trying to get to put labels on things, despite the fact that I lived in another country, and the other an Oxford-Brookes student (he unfortunately shared my name) whom I had met in the aftermath. Leaving for the trip, I left the prospect of a future with either solidly behind, which was a pity, because marrying a European always seemed, to a poor grad student at least, the most surefire way to free health care.

Luckily, it was nothing but blue skies as I entered the Peach State. Georgia was a state I had often passed through on family drives from Illinois to Florida, and I was excited to spend time there. My first stop was Milledgeville (population 18,738). I had heard about the town from Angie who was up for a teaching job at a local college there. She had told me about the troubles that had descended upon the town when its main economic engine—Central State Hospital, once the largest mental institution in the world—was shut down. I met up with the city planner, Jacob. Jacob was an imposing man with a warm demeanor—I soon learned he took on the role of the Polar Express conductor on a seasonal trolly ride for local kids. Jacob pulled a Kachen—like the mayor of Gambier, he told me the only way to understand the city is to drive around. We jumped in his car, and he took me to the abandoned campus of the Central State Hospital. Over 2,000 acres of gorgeous buildings stood empty and dilapidated as Jacob described how he was trying to help Milledgeville reinvent itself.

"My grandparents lived here. They raised my parents, who in turn raised me," he said as we drove past a decaying Georgian building. "I want to do everything I can to keep my kids here. So they can raise their kids here."

He drove me to a graveyard, where over 25,000 markers signified the patients who were buried in unmarked graves during the tenure of the asylum. The place was like the set of a horror movie, but Jacob continued to describe his attempts to draw new businesses to Milledgeville. Returning to his office, it was hard looking at it the same, knowing the abandoned horror set sitting a mile away down the road.

I left Milledgeville and drove to Savannah (population 145,403). After walking around the historic downtown with cobblestoned streets, churches, and Paula Dean restaurants, I booked myself an Airbnb on the outskirts of town. I was staying in a rental house with other guests—a family of four from Quebec and two college boys on Christmas break. The Canadians cooked me rice and chicken and talked about their own road trip throughout the United States.

"The diversity in this country," said the husband, looking at his wife for affirmation, "is unlike anything I've seen in Canada."

I was exhausted, so I retired to my room off the entryway. Sitting on my computer and planning my next steps, I was surprised to see a text from Paul. Paul had been at Northwestern a few years above me and, as someone heavily involved in student government, we always seemed to bump into each other at various events. (I can't remember if I ever voted for him.) I didn't know him that well, but I had always admired him—the kind of driven, buttoned up persona that someone of my chaotic, wing-it methodologies found appealing. He had seen that I was taking my trip on social media and reached out with an invite to a luncheon with a speaker that a local conservative group in West Palm Beach, Florida was hosting. Feeling that excellent scheduling didn't usually fall into my lap this easily, it felt like too good of an opportunity to pass up.

The next day, I hopped in Belinda and drove seven hours down to the event. I arrived dead tired and in a suit; I was annoyed to discover Paul, who was one of the managers of the event, paid me cursory attention. Did he not realize how far I had driven to get here? There was also some awkwardness about whether or not my ticket, which I had understood to be free, would or would not cost me $50. Paul eventually smoothed it out, but I still felt as though I now owed something to the group.

As I listened to a very boring speech by a writer who lamented that students were now examining race issues rather than reading Chaucer's 1387 hit *The Canterbury Tales*, I ate a wilted salad and looked at the faces sitting in the audience. As far as I could tell, most of them were wearing Brooks Brothers. All of them were white.

On my way out of the luncheon, I curtly thanked Paul as the attendees gushed over the bravery of the author, defending the sanctity of Chaucer. When I was out on the sidewalk, I heard a voice calling out. It was Paul.

"Hey!" he said, running after me in his crisp white shirt. "Those salads didn't do it for me. Me and my friend Kyle are going to get pizza. Do you want to join?"

I had driven all this way, so I got into Paul's car and joined them for a second lunch. We made casual conversation about my trip and discussed the unique brand of Florida conservatism. Kyle peeled off, and Paul decided to drive me to the vacation home that the Kennedys spent winters in. We took a photo, and Paul went back to work.

I was planning a six-hour trip up to Tallahassee where a friend from the 2016 campaign now worked as a legislative aide to a state senator. I had gone out of my way for this disappointing luncheon. It was nearly four o'clock, and I was planning to get in before 11. Before I left, I got a text from Paul asking if I would like to have dinner since we didn't get a chance to properly "catch up." Feeling I had already sunk cost by driving all the way down here, I put my plans on hold, postponing a long drive further into the night. We met up at an outdoor food market an hour later.

Sitting outside the market on a cushioned bench, we balanced sushi rolls on our knees. I could tell Paul was agitated as he made polite small talk. Only after I suggested we order a drink did he finally admit what I assumed was the reason he asked me to dinner.

"I recently came out to my family," he finally admitted with a pained expression.

"Oh, wow," I said, watching the cosmos realign.

"I'm still a Christian. I mean, I know Jesus loves me, but..." he trailed off, pushing his dark hair back. "Yeah, it's just been really tough."

Paul went on to talk about his parents and their lack of acceptance. Despite the fact that some in his family had gotten pregnant before marriage, they were not understanding of his break with "sexual morality." The hypocrisy made me seethe, but I could tell that this was a person who needed someone to confide in, not someone to start rants against the moral majority. I remember the first time I ever smoked pot; while my own friends were enjoying Fritos dipped in ice cream, I was reckoning with the concept of eternal damnation and shame. Shame was an unwelcome companion for gay men, one that could be deadly and one that was nearly impossible to shake. This shame, latent within me, was suddenly unleashed, causing me to identify with the strife Paul was experiencing. Instead of blaming those who injected these beliefs into my consciousness, I launched into my own personal faith journey with my sexuality. I told him how my parents and brother had come to be not just tolerant, but fully supportive. I spoke of how many Christian denominations were able to reconcile homosexuality as supported by the teachings of Christ. Paul seemed relieved to hear that my experience wasn't a calamity. As the sun set, he continued to describe anxieties, and I continued to offer some semblance of hope. Finally, when I saw light return to his face, I realized just how dark it was outside.

"I'm so sorry to do this, but I have a six-hour drive ahead of me..."

"It's okay!" he said, giving me a quick hug, buttoning himself up again. "It's just really nice to have someone to talk to."

Because of the delay, I stayed the night in a hotel in Gainesville, halfway between Tallahassee and Palm Beach County. Kasey, my

105

friend from the Hillary campaign, had set me up to interview a state senator and a state representative the next day. I woke up early to complete the drive, and when I arrived at the Florida capitol, I met Kasey in her boss's office. Kasey was driven and no-nonsense, and her efficiency was on full display as she had full interviews penned in the legislators' calendars. Both women were Democrats and in the minority. Jennifer Webb and Lori Berman gave frank discussions of what governing looked like with an obstructionist Republican majority, and the difficulties that came with the necessity of focusing on elections every two years. I thought about what I had learned about elections in Florida; I remembered my time working on the Hillary campaign fondly, as it had introduced me to some of my closest friends and confidants, and in some ways was an impetus for my disenchantment with the state of our politics on both sides of the aisle. As Kasey and I reminisced, we remembered one particular day as a turning point.

It was October 26, 2016, right before the Hillary Clinton/Donald Trump matchup. Even though it was fall, the Florida heat was oppressive on that dusty afternoon at Palm Beach State College where we were holding a birthday rally for our candidate. I was being sworn at, cried to, and pleaded with for bottles of water. The afternoon sun was reaching its peak, blazing down on the sprawling queue of people who had expected to be inside the rally seeing the next President of the United States.

The Palm Beach County staff were told about the rally the week of the event, and it was exactly the kick we needed as we prepared to cross the finish line. Our region had been performing so well that the campaign had sent us staffing surveys for administration jobs in Washington, meaning that none of us were going to miss a trick at the closely-watched event. Our region's first instruction was to call every voter in our "universe," the roughly 14,000 people identified by our database as having strong Democratic leanings in the area. Hillary's campaign headquarters sent orders from their tower in

Brooklyn to our tiny roadside office adjacent to a car wash. Confirm. Confirm. Confirm. We needed to lock down commitments and numbers, so we repeatedly phoned the attendees, ensuring they were a "yes" in the RSVP column.

The next day, we called them again. Just to check that they were coming.

The next day, we called them back.

When the day of the event arrived, all of us on staff turned up bleary-eyed in the college parking lot at dawn. We were expecting crowds in the high thousands now that word had spread. Hundreds of people had already gathered to get the best glimpse of Hillary. The sun was ascending, lighting the cloudless Florida sky with an optimistic glow. It was going to be a beautiful day. As I walked towards the football stadium, I said to my boss, "lucky we're going to have such nice weather today."

She shrugged. "Doesn't matter either way. The rally's in the gymnasium." She was referring to an indoor basketball court not much larger than that of a midsize public high school.

I didn't understand. "But that only seats a thousand people."

She shook her head. "Eight hundred. The stage takes up a lot of space."

I looked back at the ever-growing line. "So why the hell did we invite five-figure crowds if less than a tenth are going to get in?"

She stared as though the answer was obvious. "The news coverage. We want to show really big lines outside of the event. Show that people are excited about Hillary."

I felt tricked. Over the past few months, I had become close with my volunteers, the Floridians who gave their time without pay. In line, I saw Chip and Debbie, who made calls to show solidarity with their gay son in Ft. Lauderdale. I saw Kim, who rode the bus an hour every day to do one door knocking shift, even though she was on disability. I saw Elaine and Karen, an older couple who did all the paperwork and data entry. The people I had personally invited weren't just my region's volunteer leaders—after all the hours spent together, I considered them friends and colleagues. I had convinced them to pledge hundreds of volunteer hours for the cause, and now they would be waiting in line for an event I knew they would not be able to attend. All for what? Optics?

I was right about one thing. It was definitely a beautiful Florida day. It was also becoming an extremely hot, beautiful Florida day. Our job was now to convince the antsy crowd to sign up for volunteer shifts (and if they didn't, they would certainly be contacted by text, email, or phone until they did). One question was burned into my ears: "Am I going to see Hillary?"

I couldn't bring myself to lie. "I hope so. I really do."

As morning turned to afternoon, my impassioned pitch to sign up for volunteer shifts continued. By this time, we had run out of water, and I had overheard the phrase "heat stroke" more than a handful of times. I called out people in the crowd and explained the importance of every vote in Florida, but the heat was unbearable, and I was starting to be interrupted by people who saw the way the tide was turning. It seemed others, like me, had forgotten sunscreen, and I felt the end of my nose beginning to burn as family after family asked about their chances of getting inside. As the afternoon wore on, people became angrier and angrier, and as they shouted at me, I found myself agreeing with them.

"You called me five times. You emailed me twice. I RSVPed each time. I've been out here waiting in the sun since eight a.m. I asked if I'd get in, and you said yes. If you told me no, it would've been fine, I would've left," a woman said, tears in her eyes. "This is why people don't like politics!"

I nodded. "You're right. It's messed up." That's not what I was trained to say.

It was two o'clock, and the sun was at full power when the campaign finally devised a strategy to placate angry voters.

"The overflow section!" my boss gleefully announced. "You can watch Hillary talk on a big projection screen right outside the venue! It'll be just like being inside."

This was met with jeers from the crowd.

"I could've stayed home and watched her on TV, you idiot!"

"Do you realize how much a day off costs me?"

However, soon even the overflow section was overflowed. Eight hundred had made it inside. Five hundred made it into the overflow section. There were thousands of people left outside the event who had waited hours for nothing. I couldn't think of who was to blame. Was Brooklyn's decision to lure these people here cynical, or was it just a poorly thought-out policy? Was it the advance team's fault for refusing to level with people, or was it my fault for following orders rather than telling the voters to go home? The arms of the bureaucracy were confusing to me, even though I was a part of it. One thing was certain: the needs of the people on the ground were not the campaign's main priority.

By mid-afternoon, Hillary made a brief sweep outside to acknowledge those remaining overflow voters. Then she returned inside, and the rally began without them. The doors were firmly shut. The organizers were not invited into the rally, though we saw from Instagram that campaign leadership—absent for the past few hours—had miraculously snagged spots inside right next to the stage amidst a sea of signs declaring "I'm with her," as if to further remind those outside that they were not.

While there were greater issues in our democracy than rallies gone wrong, I thought about the disconnect that existed in our politics. It was more about whipping up excitement in campaigns than governing. Those in power were removed from what it was like to pay bills, drive their own cars, deal with changes in the price of goods. As I stood on the ground at the rally, barred from entry from the selective event, I knew that my allegiance would always be with the people outside, those without the connections to bypass the line of thousands.

After Tallahassee, I had to make an ironic backtrack. Because my brother was flying into Miami from medical school in the Caribbean for the Christmas holiday, and I had already agreed that I would pick him up, I was now doubling back towards Paul's neck of the woods. Since I was making the seven-hour drive back, I decided to check in with Paul who lived just north in Ft. Lauderdale to continue our conversation cut short by my drive to Tallahassee. We made dinner plans the night before my brother's flight arrived. I figured I could either crash on Paul's couch or grab a cheap Airbnb for the evening.

After another difficult drive through Florida, I arrived at Paul's apartment. He buzzed me up, and I sat in his living room as he dressed for dinner. He was running late from a client meeting.

I tried to make myself at home as he ran in and out of the bathroom, white button-up shirt open.

"Where do you want to go?"

"You said you'd never been to Miami. We gotta go," he said, spraying on cologne.

I made a deliberate move not to leave any of my belongings at his place. I didn't want to seem like I was setting a trap.

We drove down to dinner in Miami; we ate at an Asian fusion cafe near a dock and made small talk about the Miami area. When Paul brought up the question of where I was staying, I quickly tried to take the pressure off.

"I can find a place to stay," I said. "No worries."

"I just didn't want to, you know, assume," he said awkwardly. "I didn't want you to think I—"

"Not at all."

"I mean my couch is open if you want it. I just didn't want you to think that's why I…"

"How about this," I finally said. "I'll get dinner. That's less than I would spend to stay somewhere else."

"Deal." Paul grinned, showing dazzling teeth.

We ended the night with a drive around Miami, parking and walking into historic hotels and admiring the architecture. Paul regaled me with stories of celebrities that had visited each one; I had never seen him so animated.

Finally, he pulled into a neighborhood on an inlet. "This is my favorite neighborhood in all of Miami," he said as he parked the car. He walked up to a new craftsman house with an amazing view of the ocean. "This is the type of place I'd want to live. Big enough for a family, but still has a view of the ocean."

When we returned to Paul's apartment, I took my place on the couch. He came out from his room in pajama bottoms and gave me a pillow and blanket.

"You're good?"

"Perfect. Thank you so much, Paul."

"I just moved in, and I don't have curtains yet, so it gets really bright in the morning."

I assured him that was not a problem, but ten minutes later he called out from the bedroom and offered the other side of his bed.

"Only if you want!" he backpedaled. "I just can't sleep."

"Are you sure?"

I wasn't loving the couch to be honest.

"Totally!"

We laid four feet apart in the bedroom, talking like we were having a kid sleepover. He asked me questions about my coming out journey that I hadn't been asked in years. Suddenly, I—pejoratively referred to as "Nebraska" by drag queens in New York—was the expert. We never got closer than four feet, but somehow the pre-sleep conversations created something more wholesome, more satisfying than anything physical.

The next day, I left Paul's apartment early in the morning to pick up my brother Andrew at the Miami Airport. In the living room, the curtainless windows lit the room with blinding light. I was very glad I had not slept out there, I decided.

In my haste to get to the airport, I had forgotten to get gas. I retrieved my brother from the busy airport, and as we left Miami and began to drive across the state through Alligator Alley, I was so busy catching up with him that I missed the sign that advertised the last chance to get gas before the 50 miles of marshland. Only when we were halfway across the exitless road did see I Belinda's gas icon illuminate.

"Shit," my brother and I both said together. I looked down at my phone, which didn't have service.

The road was getting dark in front of us. I typed "gas" into Belinda's glitchy navigation system. Apparently, there was one gas station within the 20 miles of fuel we had left, but when we finally got a touch of service, Google Maps listed it as "permanently closed."

Forced to make a decision between the slight chance that there was a functioning gas station and driving down the highway until we ran out of gas, we exited the highway onto a desolate country road. We drove, watching Belinda's drivable miles go into the single digits. As we approached where the gas station allegedly stood, we held our breath, trying to come up with contingency plans.

"If we stay in the car, alligators can't get us, right?" I asked my brother.

"I heard a story about a giant snake that got into someone's engine and came in through the air conditioning," Andrew said, eyes wide.

"Well, screenshot our location so mom and dad can come find us if necessary," I said, trying to keep my voice even.

As we contemplated a night in the car hiding from reptiles, an open and fully functional Mobile gas station sign mercifully loomed ahead of us in the darkness. It was luckily not a mirage.

We arrived in Boca Grande (population 1,705) to stay with my grandparents. I was happy to see them; my grandmother is one of my personal heroes. She was an outspoken liberal, and I remembered her speaking her mind against the Iraq War to me when I was a fifth grader. When I made a disparaging remark about something being "gay" at the age of 10, she forcefully told me off. In the early

2000s, she was probably one of the only adults I knew with the moral compass to do so.

The day after we arrived back in Boca Grande for the Christmas holidays, I got a text from Paul asking if he could come visit Boca Grande. He was working in real estate, and he explained how he loved to travel around the state, looking at houses for design ideas. Whether or not this was the primary reason, I was looking forward to it. I felt that we were one step away from something, whatever it was, and this would probably be the only chance to advance the plot if it was meant to be advanced.

The next day, Paul showed up at my grandparents' house in Florida, wielding flowers for them in his arms. We had lunch in town and I suggested the idea of renting kayaks so he could get a view of the houses.

We rented the long blue kayak and dragged it from downtown to the beach. We pushed off from the shore and fought against a wake that was rougher than it seemed from the beach. We paddled north towards the largest beach houses. Looking at the rows of mansions on the north end of the island, I watched Paul look at them hungrily. I knew he was in South Florida heaven.

"Can we pull up to shore?" he asked.

"I don't see why not," I said, paddling my way towards the beach.

We pulled the kayak onto the sand. We disembarked from the plastic boat and walked up to one of the towering mansions surrounded by tropical trees.

"This is the one," he said excitedly. Paul showed very little fear as he trespassed onto a wooden path leading to the property. I followed him tentatively.

I found him standing next to the house. His eyes sparkled as he looked up at the sun dancing on the windows of the empty mansion. "Let's pretend this is our house," he said, looking at it longingly.

"Oh, it definitely is," I said, laughing.

He turned around and looked at me, almost quizzically. I was trying to figure out if he was tan because he lived in Florida year-round or if that was his natural pigmentation, but I realized it probably looked like I was staring.

"I'm really glad I'm here," he said as he stepped towards me.

"Well, you should be here," I said, motioning up to the mansion. "It's your house."

He didn't smile. He moved toward me like he had made a decision. As his face got close to mine, I closed my eyes. A seagull cawed and we kissed.

We lingered for a moment, then he pulled away and opened his eyes. He looked like he was in a state of disbelief.

"Was that okay?" I asked, laughing nervously.

"Yeah," he said quietly, almost to himself. "It's just that…"

An eagle flew overhead. He looked up and tracked its progress across the sky.

"What?"

He looked back to me, almost defensively, like I was going to pull a trick on him. "That was my first kiss," he said quietly.

I wasn't prepared for that. I tried to keep my surprise under wraps. "First one… with a guy or…?"

He shook his head and looked out over the horizon. "Ever."

The significance of that moment for Paul hit me. I stood next to him and put an arm on his back. I wasn't sure what to say, or ask. A first kiss was a concept that seemed foreign to me.

"I'm glad it was a good one," he said, after a moment.

I looked over at him, trying to gauge his state of mind.

"You deserve a good one," was all I could say.

I felt an incredible responsibility to curate the moment: I knew we were on a knife's edge between this experience being extraordinary or cringeworthy. But I couldn't find the words to say. Instead, we stood and looked out over the horizon for a moment until the waves got dangerously close to pulling our kayak out to the ocean.

THE DEEP SOUTH

I TOOK time off from my travels for Christmas and the New Year. I was feeling energized and refreshed as I was diving into what I assumed would be the most difficult part of the journey. I began my trip again from Mobile, Alabama (population 184,952). There I stayed with Kathleen, an artist and mother of Cat, a friend of mine I'd met as a fellow American in the UK. Cat had planned on driving through her native Alabama and Mississippi with me but had been sidetracked going into the New Year. I was now going alone.

This was okay, however. Paul and I had made plans to meet up in one of the states I was visiting in the next few weeks. I was feeling as though we were trending in a positive direction, enough for him to travel and spend time with me and enough for me to rearrange my schedule to see if this was something that could end up going somewhere.

I arrived and found Kathleen—a fiery and diminutive woman with blonde hair—standing outside of her Mobile, Alabama home, ready to welcome me. When I got a chance to get my bearings, I found that she had taken a personal interest in the project and had arranged for a full-on tour of Mobile.

We started our tour of Mobile at the Mardi Gras Museum. The curator, a well-tanned man in a suit who was around my age, showed took me through rooms of well-preserved parade floats, masks, and debutante gowns. He was adamant that I understand that Mardi Gras originated in Mobile; Alabama was the real home of something we all attributed to New Orleans.

"It was ours first," he said, fists clenched. Something like genuine rage was bubbling underneath. I decided not to mention that New Orleans was where I was headed next.

Kathleen took me to meet a friend, Tina, for dinner at Wintzell's Oyster House where we had delicious fried fish, fries, and pickles with sweet tea. I was firmly enjoying my time in The South, and I began asking about the community.

"We take care of our own here," she said. "Through the church, yes, but also through what we know is expected of us."

Kathleen went on to tell me how her family had their home in Southern Mississippi destroyed in Hurricane Katrina. "It wasn't just New Orleans, you have to remember that," she said. "New Orleans gets all the attention."

Her friend scoffed and nodded in agreement.

Note to self: don't bring up New Orleans in Mobile, Alabama.

"Part of the reason this community means so much to me is the care they showed our family when we came here. We had nothing, and I mean *nothing*," she paused for effect, "besides what we could fit in our car when we fled."

"The community makes you feel held," Tina said. "And when you have a strong community, you don't need government."

They went on to good-naturedly try to convince me I was a closet Republican.

Of course, I knew that the pasts of places like Mobile couldn't be ignored. It was easy for me to wander in and be welcomed with open arms by a certain echelon of society, one that participated in debutante balls and was connected to Mardi Gras museums. But thus far, I was feeling held by the community in the South, a community that really wanted me to see the best of them. But I also had to admit that being white opened certain doors.

I wondered if it was Southern hospitality or a need for someone from the other persuasion to see the good she saw in her own community when Kathleen introduced me to Ntunze, an African refugee whom she had personally helped assimilate into Mobile society.

Ntunze told her story of moving to Alabama after living in a refugee camp in Tanzania.

"The first time on the plane, I was so happy. Because I'm going to America," Ntunze said, eyes glistening under her head scarf.

Kathleen interjected to detail how Catholic Social Services had helped make their assimilation easier.

"So the purpose of his visit is to find out how… maybe how people are kinder? People are nice here. It doesn't matter for me if you're from Lebanon, you're from Africa or Mississippi." She looked to Ntunze for affirmation. "I mean, don't you feel that way?"

I spoke on the phone with Paul that night. We decided to meet in Tennessee; I would alter my schedule so I could stay four days with him there, meaning that I would have to truncate my time in the Deep South to get there on time, and that I would have to have a more cursory experience of the three states than I would've liked. I was giddy at the prospect of finding not only a travel buddy, but perhaps a companion beyond the travels. As we planned where we would meet, I had hoped to spend time in a small town. I sent him an inexpensive cabin in a remote area of Tennessee I found on Airbnb. I felt his trepidation over the phone; maybe I was giving off murderer vibes? He responded with some more upscale options in Nashville where the art was color-coordinated with the bedding. I got a sense that he was choosy and wasn't ready to slum it the way I had been. I was cheap; he was not. Opposites attract, I decided. I put down a deposit on the place, trying not to think about my ballooning credit card debt.

I took off the next day towards New Orleans. I was supposed to stay with a campaign friend, Betsy, who was there on a girls' trip with friends from college. That is, until I got a text from her when I was an hour outside of town.

"My friends don't feel comfortable with you staying with us."

I was horrified. What was it about me?

"They don't know you. You're a strange boy."

I definitely was a strange boy, but I had never been described as putting people on edge before.

"Well can I come and meet them and see what they think then?"

A pause. "Sure."

I drove to New Orleans (population 376,971), hoping I could win them over.

I arrived and parked my car in a garage. I texted them, asking where they were.

"At dinner."

"Okay, where?"

No response. I decided to walk down Bourbon Street. I posted on Instagram. "In New Orleans! Know anyone I could hang out with?"

Sure enough, within the hour, I was at a bar with a friend of a friend from Chicago. Keisha was a former actress and self-proclaimed psychic medium.

"I moved to New Orleans after I realized I could communicate with the dead," she said over a frozen coffee cocktail.

"Oh!" I said, choking on my drink. This was my first time meeting a psychic. "Tell me about that."

She explained how she had communicated with a spirit in an apartment in Chicago two years ago. She had allegedly solved a murder in the apartment that had taken place in the 1920s. (She didn't elaborate if justice was served through the legal system.) She was so changed by the experience that she had moved to New

Orleans to pursue her dream of being a full-time psychic. She now worked in a crystal shop.

My mind was wandering as I watched my phone to see if I would indeed have a place to stay that night. As Keisha explained how a rival crystal shop owner had put a curse on her and how she met a little boy in that shop whom she believed to be her son from the future sent to connect with her, I realized I was probably not going to hear from my friend Betsy. I excused myself to the restroom, and I reached out to the parents of my friend from college, asking if I could stay with them a night earlier than expected. They quickly agreed and told me not to rush, telling me their doors were open anytime.

I returned from the bathroom more at ease, having secured a place to stay. I listened with less anxiety as Keisha explained her new life in New Orleans and found my reflexive skepticism turned to amused curiosity. She believed in her abilities so much that she had uprooted her whole life and moved across the country. She was on her own journey too.

I arrived at the lovely historic home of Jocelyn and Mark on Moss Street near the canals just outside the city. It was a towering, historic home that had withstood decades of changes in the city, including Hurricane Katrina. Mark, a doctor with a kind face, and Jocelyn, a lovely woman with boundless energy, quickly welcomed me in and showed me incredible hospitality. When I told them about my experience with Keisha, I expected them to share my amusement. Rather, they treated the story as if I was describing drinks with a banker.

"Haunted is sort of in the water here in New Orleans," Jocelyn said, looking around the house. "Everyone has stories of odd things like that: footsteps in the middle of the night, lights going on without explanation—things like that."

I went to sleep that night skeptical, but sure enough, at three in the morning I was awoken by the sound of a door slamming.

Whether or not Mark and Jocelyn did this simply to welcome me to the city, I'll never know.

The food in New Orleans is famously good and did not disappoint. Mark and Jocelyn took me out for a lovely seafood dinner and described New Orleans as a "thin place," or somewhere considered to have an easier connection between the living and the dead. As we drove home past above-ground tombs and mausoleums, I felt the impact of a city that was infused with a sense of mortality.

In Baton Rouge (population 222,185), I stopped by Parrain's Seafood Restaurant, sat at the bar, and ordered some gator bites. When the bartender realized I was alone, he struck up a friendly conversation. I told him it was my first time in Baton Rouge, and he returned with a sampler of their best fried shrimp and oysters. I was appreciative; I was not yet used to the rhythms of being on my own without a guide. Soon, a woman down the bar and her husband started to converse with me. They too were from the Midwest, 20 miles from Rockford actually, and they had moved to Louisiana over a decade ago. "Best decision we ever made," they told me. I thought about myself in the state of Louisiana. I considered how foreign not only the history was, but the unwritten rules of a community. How long would it take for me to learn them? Would I ever be able to fully understand them?

I drove through Mississippi and stopped in Jackson where I met up with the author of *Dispatches From Pluto: Lost and Found in the Mississippi Delta*, Richard Grant. Grant was a British author whose book I had listened to on my drive, and I was enchanted by the tale of Grant buying a house with his wife in the backwoods of Mississippi and the adventures that came with it. When I arrived at Grant's house in the suburbs of Jackson, we decided to walk around his neighborhood. Grant, a bearded man with graying hair, talked about the culture shock of leaving small-town Mississippi in favor of the capital city.

"I'm used to parties where people are shooting off cannons and jumping out of planes."

"Actually?"

"Oh yes," he said, looking nostalgic. "It's weird to get accustomed to dinner parties where people just talk about golf and lawn care."

I felt I was doing myself a disservice, missing out on the smaller towns across the South. I explained my guilt to Grant that I had to change my schedule because I was on my way to see a romantic prospect.

He seemed to get it. "Journeys aren't just about interviewing mayors."

I finally arrived in Nashville to meet Paul with excitement and trepidation. A part of me felt a little silly; we had known each other tangentially for such a long period of time, yet the intimacy of spending a week together in a new city was thrilling and a little embarrassing because of how quickly things had happened. I felt reckless as I sat in Nashville traffic, and even more so because of my hope that I would find answers I was looking for.

I pulled up to an Airbnb that was built above a garage in the back of an immaculate home in a nice area of Nashville. It was by far the nicest place I had stayed yet on the trip (that wasn't the home of someone letting me crash). I parked off the alley and waited for him to arrive. Fifteen minutes later, he pulled into the driveway, immaculate teeth and sunglasses glinting.

As he got out of the car and hugged me, I immediately sensed the doubts behind the grin.

"This is really happening," Paul said, a little breathlessly.

"Yeah," I said, trying my best to muster a reassuring smile. The complexity of the situation was creeping up on me. The awkwardness of plans that had been made in hasty excitement over the phone one night were suddenly here in plain daylight. There was so much complexity in two men arriving at an Airbnb in the South, one of whom had only recently come out, the other with no permanent address. It was one thing to be a romantic; it was another to be reckless.

Paul opened his mouth, maybe to acknowledge exactly what I was thinking. Unfortunately, at that moment, the owner of the house, a woman who oozed moneyed frantic energy, came out to welcome us to her spare property.

"Okay, who is Ryan?"

I raised my hand.

"So… it's you staying here, right?"

Correct. "Yep."

She turned to Paul. "And who is this?"

"This is the second guest."

That hung in the air for a moment. I didn't know if I was projecting judgment into the lull, but I knew Paul was.

"Okay! So the door uses an app to unlock, you'll need to download that…"

After what felt like a lifetime, our frazzled host let us into the space. It was a cozy apartment built above a garage, a one room bedroom/living room combo. With its pitched roof, the space felt oddly…

"Churchlike, don't you think?" Paul said, instantly gravitating towards the design elements we were paying premium prices for. There was some awkwardness as he unpacked his bags. The man had never been kissed, and suddenly we were playing house in a small backyard Airbnb, preparing for dinner downtown.

We went to downtown Nashville and had a nice dinner at a trendy pan-Asian restaurant. While we were trying to keep the atmosphere buoyant, his unease was apparent, and my guilt at not doing more hard-hitting journalism was starting to seep into my consciousness.

We returned, turned on the film *Chocolat*, and sat in bed together. As someone who had shared beds with friends on the trip, this time didn't feel much different. I wasn't feeling excitement anymore. I was feeling that indescribable feeling of becoming aware that you've made the wrong choice but trying to find a way to cover it up. If only I pushed through, made the right joke, or changed my mindset, things would be better. I looked across the bed at Paul. He looked back at me and smiled again. It was an empty smile, like newscaster's grin. Was he feeling the same regret I was? I turned away and went to sleep.

I woke up accepting that maybe things weren't meant to work out, but this made me even more set on making my time in Tennessee count. I suggested that we visit the Tennessee state capitol building that day. By pure coincidence, we arrived at the capitol building the next afternoon while the 2019 legislators were being inaugurated. To my dismay, Paul had decided to participate by becoming my personal photographer, and one of the state legislators noticed Paul photographing me and him in the same shot.

"What the hell's going on here?" Rep. Joe Towns Jr. said as he approached me dressed in a dark suit with a pink tie.

I briefly explained what I was doing with my 50 states trip. The representative gave me his card and asked me to email his secretary to arrange an interview. Feeling celebratory, we went to a bougie donut shop on our way back to get recording equipment.

"You know," Paul said, "I love seeing what you're doing."

"Really?"

"It's more of a hustle than I realized it was."

"It's not all designer donuts," I said.

"I'd like to join you again. For another part of the trip. Maybe California?" He flashed his grin.

"You know, I just want to say, I realize I'm on this manic dash across the country," I said, studying his face, "but I was always planning on taking things slow."

He nodded. "People do move slow in California too."

I thought of my plans for the West Coast. Maybe I could make it work.

Paul decided to come along with me for the adventure to the capitol. Unsure of what to tell him to do during the interview, I left him in the lobby as I took the elevator up to the legislative offices.

Joe welcomed me into his book-lined office. He sat me down and immediately started to monologue about the state of the country, creating a patchwork of historical and modern examples as he described his journey from working on other people's campaigns to becoming a legislator himself. I pivoted to some of his early statements about how the country had changed.

"You just mentioned that the country is different now than it was 40 years ago. In what ways do you see that?"

He looked at me quizzically. "You said 40 years ago?"

"I can't remember what number you said," I replied, my mind still elsewhere.

"I didn't give a number. I think you're trying to be cute. Are you trying to age me?"

"You look younger than 40," I said. I was off my game today.

"But no, actually, you're right. Obviously, the country is better in a lot of ways. The racial strife is better than what it was. However, racism is still rearing its hideous head again with these knucklehead groups. But, we've made progress. And I think that in the white community, white people are more apt and aggressive to fight this than they were 50 years ago. White people are not afraid to fight that crap. Say there's a Klan march. You'll find white people to march against that crap. Okay. All right, that's a good thing. That's progress. So what that is, that's courage."

He sighed and took a dramatic lean back in his chair. "But."

I leaned in, holding my microphone.

"I had an opportunity to be with Joe Biden maybe three months ago. He's at the Orpheum Theater in Memphis, Tennessee. And he said, 'I thought we had taken care of those problems. Problems of people having the right to vote. I thought we'd taken care of those problems of race and these kinds of things that you see popping up today.'"

"So history is repeating itself in some ways?"

"The point being, yes, the country dealt with those things at that particular time. However, ugliness and diabolical activity never goes to sleep. It's never permanently put out of business, which means that people have to always be vigilant. Yes, we dealt with it, but there's another crew being bred because of the evil and iniquity that lies in human beings. Yes, it was taken care of. But not permanently. So young guys and gals of goodwill have to always be ready to fight for what's right."

Rep. Joe Towns's cell phone rang. I began to put away my recording equipment.

"What are you doing now?"

I thought of Paul roaming the hallways. "Probably going to go out to some spots downtown."

"There's an inauguration party tonight at the Hermitage Hotel. I'll be spending time with the Congressional Black Caucus. You ought to come."

"Okay," I said, immediately thinking of what clothing I had.

"7 p.m. And you can bring that creepy picture-taking friend of yours."

I left the office and found Paul wandering through the halls. "We're going to a party tonight."

We spent the night at the party, where I felt extremely honored and confused to be present with the entire Congressional Black

Caucus. Before the party, Joe and other Congressional leaders made speeches and introduced up-and-coming members. At the party, Rep. Towns introduced me to other legislators, and introduced Paul as my assistant, which I could tell irritated Paul.

The night ended with Joe Towns and a crew of other legislators sitting around after the party. There was a new urgency in the way he addressed me.

"You're traveling through the South. What do you think?"

"Everyone has been so kind to me. The hospitality has been... well, just like this. Everywhere I go."

Towns nodded. "I don't want you to be leaving here without understanding the history. Do you understand me?"

He began to dive into a variety of historical anecdotes, weaving a tapestry of stories of oppression in the South, from the Tuskegee experiments in Alabama to the mayor of Memphis meeting with Black faith leaders clutching a shotgun in his hand.

"I heard the sound of the shot that killed Dr. King. I just want you to remember. Evil people are still abound. Okay. All over the world, not just in this country, but all over the world. And I believe that those things that we as a country had dealt with seem to be resurfacing."

My time with Rep. Joe Towns was optimistic but mixed with a warning. America was making progress, but evil very much lived under the surface.

The last night in Nashville, Paul and I found a honky-tonk party at an American Legion Hall. For some reason, I felt some trepidation arriving as two men to an event, but I needn't have worried. The clientele in the place did skew older, but I was charmed to see a group of goth teenage girls tearing it up on the dance floor and inviting men in their eighties to join them. Paul and I bought pitchers of beer and laughed with the older couple at our table, retired professors from the University of Tennessee system.

The fact it was the last night meant that Paul and I returned home with some expectations. Like everything on the trip thus far, I felt I had to find some meaning in it. Our relationship, which had gone from zero to sixty so quickly in December, now felt stalled. I thought I suspected the reason why, but after a few drinks I felt I had the courage to finally come out and see if I had diagnosed the tension lingering between us. Paul and I were lying in bed. I figured that if I didn't ask, I'd never understand whether it was my actions or Paul's own struggles that had caused the awkwardness over the past few days. The weekend felt almost punishingly platonic.

We laid in bed, neither of us able to sleep. Before I could start my monologue diagnosing what had gone wrong, Paul turned to me and asked, "Are you upset?"

I was surprised by the frankness of the question. "I think that depends."

He looked intently back. "On what?"

"The reason this has all unfolded like this."

"I'm just not… I don't think I'm ready for…"

He looked down at the bed. I was horrified.

"You think I wanted to… I told you I was okay with taking things slow!"

He looked sheepish. "I didn't know what kind of expectations you had…"

"You saw how seriously I took it that I was your first kiss. Don't you think I want to be respectful here? Did you really think I wanted this trip to be your first time?"

"Well…" Paul looked aghast. "It wouldn't be my first time."

I looked at him like he had just revealed he played in the NBA. "What?"

"Well not *fully* my first time," Paul continued. "Just like… stuff happened. One time. In a hot tub."

Unkindly, I found myself laughing. "Okay, not *quite* what I was expecting."

The look on his face confirmed that laughing was the wrong thing to do.

"It's just that you… skipped a few steps," I said, trying to turn it into a joke.

But I quickly stopped laughing when I saw that his eyes were filled with tears. "Don't you know how guilty I've felt?"

What the hell happened in that hot tub?

I reached out and touched his arm. "No, seriously, I mean it when I say this is great. It's so much less pressure for me, I—"

But this was also certainly the wrong thing to say. Paul seemed tormented by what he had admitted. "Why is it less pressure for *you*?"

I wanted to explain the responsibility I had felt to treat him with care as he navigated finding himself. Instead, I found myself saying, "I seriously don't care. I actually am so relieved that you have some, I don't know, experience or whatever."

But soon, Paul launched into a monologue that I had heard many times before from many gay men. The shame he carried with him. It was so uniform, it was almost monotonous. The close-minded church, the un-affirming parents, the unaccepting friends, the homophobic comments, the fear of a complicated life, the desire to be normal. I was tired of all of it. I had found a way to make my peace with it, but I was angry that someone else was still tormented by all of these controlling lies. What started as pity for Paul turned into spite for those who imposed a worldview that I considered to be full of convenient double standards.

"I thought you were starting to see through it," I said, trying to keep the disappointment out of my voice.

"See through what?"

"It's like… they know they're peddling bullshit. They know the people who fall for the guilt are suckers."

I tried to backtrack, but the damage had been done.

"But I subscribe to that. So I'm a sucker?"

I didn't want to lie. But I saw the way he was looking at me, like

I was a heretic temptress there to corrode his worldview. And I knew that whatever beliefs he was grappling with were foundational. No amount of logic from me would change the way he felt; not here, at least. I was trying not to get worked up thinking about all of the time I had spent in self-hatred and shame while other kids were out doing whatever they felt like with impunity. All I could bring myself to say was, "Don't waste your time hating yourself, please."

And so I turned over and went to bed, but I wanted to say one last piece.

"I know that you may be afraid I see you as some…" my brain jammed, "I don't know, emotionally-stunted person, but I really do respect…"

I looked at his face. I didn't even try to backtrack. I had mishandled the whole situation. I had misjudged where he was at on his own journey, and I had lacked the tact needed to help him navigate the choppy waters of this part of his process. I knew it was over.

The next day we politely packed up the place we had called home for the past four days. I took a small bottle of the nice shampoo. We drove to a bookstore to meet up with Michael, my next travel companion, fresh from a year in Japan. We all made small talk as Paul passed the baton to Michael to keep me company on the journey. I sensed that Paul was sizing Michael up, trying to decide if Michael could handle spending time with someone as callous as me. Paul and I parted ways with a quick hug, and we made vague plans that we would, as mentioned, meet up in California. This surprising burst of romance had reinvigorated my belief that there was something tangible that would change me on the journey. We both knew we would probably never see each other again.

As I got in the car with Michael, I was so grateful for the chance to have a friend at my side, someone with whom I gladly knew where we stood. Michael, strawberry blond, perpetually curious, and filled with a goofy sort of childlike joy, was the perfect familiar foil to the unsure stranger I had spent time with in Nashville. I hoped that I would be able to shake off the disappointment of the weekend and return to the person I was when Michael and I parted ways three years prior.

Michael and I had graduated from Northwestern the same year and both decided to move out to Los Angeles. We were each other's ride or die, going out to eat noodles in Chinatown and going to bars in Echo Park and pretending to be "Simon," a timid man on his bachelor party trying to get into hijinks, a role that we would switch as the night went on, to the confusion of those we were pranking.

Michael was looking out the window like a dog during their first time in the car. "I still can't wrap my head around it."

"Being back?"

He nodded vigorously. "I'm less than a month out from living in Japan, and now I'm driving through the South with you," he said as we passed an anti-abortion billboard. "It's wild."

As I pulled onto the highway, happy to get out of Nashville, I considered how I was not the same as I was when we both lived together back in Los Angeles. How he had been changed by his time in Japan, just as I had been by my time at Oxford. As we stopped at a gas station, I wrote a quick journal entry to myself. It was the first time I was aware that my thoughts and opinions would certainly evolve, that this was just a snapshot of the person I was when I traveled across the country at this divisive moment in time. That the people I met by chance would shape me and my ideas on this trip, just as they would with whatever came after. And I, like the country I was exploring, would never be one set thing. Like my homeland, I was always evolving and changing. The sin would be not to acknowledge or be introspective about the implications of that.

. . .

Michael and I drove through the misty hills of Arkansas, stopping in Hot Springs (population 38,559), where the hot springs were closed because of the 2019 government shutdown. We settled for drinking root beer brewed with hot springs water at a local brewery before driving even farther north to visit the Clinton Presidential Library in Little Rock. This too was closed because of the shutdown. Michael and I drove past Little Rock Central High School, where the Little Rock Nine—a group of nine courageous African American students—were the first to integrate into the school system amidst a backdrop of incredible unrest in the 1950s.

We drove to Arkadelphia (population 10,670), where we stayed with the parents of a classmate from college. We arrived at a picture-perfect home right downtown; Bill and Linda were college professors with warm smiles and were some of the kindest and most generous people I'd met along the way. Both Bill and Linda were adamant about introducing me to Johnny Wink, a coworker of theirs and an English professor at Ouachita Baptist College.

"Johnny is a legend at Ouachita. He's just one of the most empathetic and amazing people you will meet on this trip," Bill said. I believed him; Bill was not a man of hyperbole. He set us up for an appointment to meet the esteemed professor.

That night, we went out to a local bar in downtown Arkadelphia. The bar was engaged in a game of Jackbox, a joke game projected on a screen but played on your phone. Quiplash was a game that challenged you to come up with the best joke answer to a prompt, a game that Michael and I had both played before. One thing I hadn't considered was how senses of humor vary by regions across the country. It became obvious there was one punchline that couldn't fail: Hillary Clinton. When the prompt "The worst thing to hear from your spouse: 'I'm leaving you for __'" came up and Monica Lewinsky was the winning answer, the chuckles across the bar at the former First Lady of Arkansas's expense egged me on to write more Killary-themed answers. On the campaign we absorbed the conspiracy theories about our candidate and frequently wove them into our sense of humor; it was how we made sense of the madness. I wrote "Hillary for Prison" and made further conspiratorial joke answers to test the room. Things that were said about the queen of the Satanist Cabal were acceptable on Twitter, but the conspiratorial jokes didn't land with the crowd. These conspiracies spread like wildfire online unchecked, but in polite company they seemed almost perverted. Maybe they were a little too real for Arkedelphians.

The following day Bill and Linda proudly gave us a tour of Ouachita Baptist College's beautiful campus, where we met Johnny Wink in his office. The office was lined with books and pictures of former students. Johnny was in his late 60s and had a gentle Arkansas accent that instantly relaxed you. He spoke, always putting my name at the end of the sentence. Launching into our talk, Johnny showed me letters from his favorite students and took me to a bulletin board with pictures of those who had kept in touch. As he talked about a student he had grown close with a decade earlier, a Black man whose wedding picture featured prominently on the bulletin board, he talked about his work fighting for the Civil Rights Movement in the 1960s and talked unabashedly about the fights he's faced for the underdogs at the university.

"Do you feel your background as a writer is where that empathy comes from?"

Johnny put a finger to his lips and leaned back in his chair.

"I don't know that for sure. I mean, I don't know exactly who I would be. I can't believe I'd be quite the same person I am because, you know, I'm thinking nurture has something to do with nature, with who you are and how we wind up, you know? I think for a lot of people on this campus, they get it into their mind that being different or having problems means you've got something wrong with you. And we can fix it. So you take something like, say, alcoholism and you say, okay, this is something wrong with you.

You've got alcoholism. We can fix you. You've got homosexuality. We can fix you."

My heart stopped. The topic was sensitive for me, and I wasn't sure what this gentle man was going to say.

"I'm thinking of all the tragedy, and I've watched this play out. I don't know why it is, but over the course of years I've been here, I've had maybe a dozen people come to me and say, 'I don't know if you're the person I ought to be talking to,' and then sit here behind closed doors and tell me, you know, 'I'm gay' and ask 'do you have any advice for being gay at Ouachita?'"

I thought of a gay student at Ouachita. Then I thought of Paul.

Johnny continued. "And you know, I'm thinking, I wish you well, because this is a difficult place. I can remember every once in a while, in the bad old days, somebody would write a letter, some student or a faculty member talking about gay people in just God-awful terms. And yeah, you know, closeted young people had to just take it."

I went to Christian schools for most of my life. Though I was a Lutheran, I attended a Catholic high school. There was a lot of agreement between the two faiths, a lot to love and aspire to. Yet, many gay members of my high school faculty ended up leaving because they felt they could not be who they were (meanwhile, straight coaches could sleep with female students on religious retreats with impunity, as was an open secret during my high school days). Lying was a sin, plain and simple, yet within our Christian schools and families, we were constantly shown that sometimes deception is not only permissible; it can be superior to the truth.

Johnny must've seen my mind working. He leaned in toward me and continued. "And I used to always write, Ryan, I mean I was like Pavlov's dog. Somebody would write a letter like that and bang, I'm coming back with a letter to the editor expressing a very different point of view. I then wrote the administration once and I said, 'Don't you think that you ought to have proof of advertisement here?' I mean, don't you think that in our promotional literature, if we're trying to get people here, don't you think that we really ought to have some little rider clause saying, 'by the way, Ouachita is not a gay-friendly place'?"

Johnny gave me a parting gift; a copy of *Blue Highways* by William Least-Heat Moon, which I treasure. As I looked at Johnny's face, something welled up inside of me after what had happened in Tennessee. The oasis of decency and empathy that existed in this office made me feel that empathetic Christianity was alive and well, and that I shouldn't be quick to paint with a broad brush.

THE SOUTHWEST

FROM ARKANSAS, Michael and I traveled to Oklahoma. We were staying with Amber, a friend of a friend whom I had met during college. Amber was a dental hygienist with the best teeth I had ever seen. We traveled to Norman (population 122,837) to stay at Amber's house just a few blocks from the University of Oklahoma campus. There we met her girlfriend Jana, who had recently moved from the Czech Republic and was a rep for a beer company in a state where, until that year, a grocery store could not sell alcohol stronger than 3.2%.

"My job is about to get a lot easier," Jana said. "America is so strange with their views on alcohol."

We ate at a small Italian cafe downtown, Victoria's. Over pasta, Amber and Jana asked some clever questions and were able to clarify that straight Michael was not, in any shape or form, my boyfriend.

After dinner, Amber and Jana introduced me to their friend Tanner who gave me a tour of the University of Oklahoma campus. The campus was one of the only examples of an architectural style that Frank Lloyd Wright called "Cherokee Gothic," which combined classic geometric patterns of the Cherokee tribe to offset the excesses of gothic architecture. As we walked through the high-ceilinged reading room at the library, I marveled at the meeting of the two cultures.

Amber and Jana took us to stay in Oklahoma City (population 643,692), a town that completely enchanted me. I felt a little kick in my gut, a little inkling that this could be the place that I settle down. As we drove through the stunning downtown, visiting a laundromat-turned-brewery and walking over a lit modern bridge, I felt my preconceived notions about Oklahoma melt away. This was a properly cosmopolitan town, and a capital city at that. We met some of Amber and Jana's friends for drinks, and, when they told me how much they paid for their house, I was even more interested. After, we decided to go downtown to visit the memorial of the Oklahoma City bombings.

As I stood looking out over the reflecting pool, I turned to Amber and admitted something.

"Is it bad I don't actually know anything about the motive for the Oklahoma City bombings?"

Amber shook her head. "A lot of people don't. There's a documentary you should see."

We went back to Jana's apartment on the outskirts of Oklahoma City and Amber queued up a documentary about the bombing. The events leading up to the bombings chilled me. It was more nebulous than evil, rather a cocktail of racial grievances, anti-government views, and conspiracy theories that one man's mind had turned from chaos into a blueprint for righteous action. As the documentary connected the dots between the standoff at Ruby Ridge, the FBI raid on the Branch Davidians in Waco, and McVeigh's influence from the apocalyptic book, *The Turner Diaries* (perhaps the most horrifying of the influences, an adventure story of an order of white supremacists wielding nuclear weapons to rid the world of inferior races—Nazism for comic nerds), I realized the sheltered life I had in Rockford, not just from physical danger, but from dangerous, paranoid thinking.

"Stochastic terrorism" is defined as "the public demonization of a person or group resulting in the incitement of a violent act, which is statistically probable but whose specifics cannot be predicted." I thought of chants of "Lock Her Up." The power of anti-government rhetoric was engrained in American history, but a unique strain had developed during my lifetime. I had grown up with FOX News warning of "death panels" from Sarah Palin during the Obamacare passage, saw the rise of the anti-government Tea Party and Freedom Caucus, and heard the wide net of demonizations from candidates on the other side of the aisle during the 2016 election. The responsibility for events like these did not lay solely on any of the individuals, but also on the culture of intentional fear-mongering by those in power. While most citizens can either ratio-nalize or absorb the fear, some would choose to act. Less than two years later, people from around the country would take lies about a stolen election and storm the United States capitol. Those who stoked paranoia were playing with dangerous fire.

I was able to have a decent night's sleep at Jana's condo before our meeting with a candidate for the Absentee-Shawnee nation Governor. We drove an hour out of Norman, past sprawling prairies behind wooden fences, towards the main administrative building of the tribe. The building was modern, contrasting the vast, dusty land sprawling for miles past it. We met with John John-son, currently a secretary for the Absentee-Shawnee tribe, in his office on the reservation. John was a man with a kind but severe face tucked behind a desk in his windowless office.

"Tell me about your main goals for your gubernatorial candidacy."

He nodded. "Economic development. That's my main goal here. We've always had projects, but they just never seem to take off. We have a gentleman that's in the tribe that has his own business. He does some small aircraft type stuff. We can take baby steps and just grow, based on that."

John went on to describe how, despite encouragement to marry from within the tribe or other tribes from elder Absentee-Shawnee members, many younger tribe members are marrying other cultures outside of the tribe because of the sheer interrelatedness of nearby reservations.

"If I wanted to date someone over here, someone would say, 'No, you can't, that's your uncle's niece' or something like that, or I'd go to a pow-wow 30 miles away and find someone there. And my grandma goes, 'Oh no, that's my nephew's daughter. You can't.' So I kind of had to lean into going to a white school."

John described how his wife was white, and I asked what that meant for tribal activities.

"There's one particular ritual dance where we had to ask white spouses to excuse themselves, cross the road for a little bit. And you know, they understand." He thought about this for a moment. "Well *mostly* understand. Like my wife says, 'those are my kids. I have your kids and now they're going to make me get out of here?' I mean, not get out. You just have to go past the road."

As we drove away from the Absentee-Shawnee headquarters, I thought of the cultural rules that people brought to relationships. Our upbringings shaped us so much, and many Americans couldn't agree on the fundamentals of our shared identity. I thought about the distortions Paul had been fed. These rules allowed certain "immoral" behaviors to be permissible for some, and other behaviors to act as a constant drain of guilt on the soul. The disintegration of the promising relationship I stumbled into had started to unravel a spool in my mind that I wasn't ready for. Was I simply hoping to conjure this perfect relationship to prove that I too was normal? That I was allowed to stake my claim on the American dream as well? I had hoped that I would have found my place in America, and yet I found myself feeling rejected from a society which set the traps of shame that Paul had fallen into.

Perhaps I was lying to myself; maybe it wasn't him I was angry with. It was myself, for how long I felt forced to deal in the currency of deceit. Finding a person to accept me as I was meant that I could show the world that I was acceptable. That all my years of trying and failing and running from myself had paid off. But now it seemed even more unlikely that I would find someone who shared not only my sense of values, but sorrow at the world we were brought up in. My desire to live a normal life was an act of defiance.

Red and blue lights were flashing in the lane next to me. A cop had pulled up next to my car, waving to get my attention. I pulled off the road instantly. I had a feeling that maybe he had been following me for much longer than I noticed.

I was right.

"Do you know how long I've been tailing you?"

My mind still unspooling, I started to babble at the highway patrolman. "I'm sorry we're in a hurry to get to Dallas. I'm traveling to all 50 states to understand democracy."

The officer stared at me, his aviators glinting in the Oklahoma sun.

"Okay. Can you do it... slower?"

I saw my eyes widen in his glasses. "Of course."

"Enjoy Texas. Drive slow."

And just like that, he walked back to his patrol car and sped back onto the highway, kicking some dust onto Belinda as he sped away.

Michael could tell I was shaken because he let me think as we kept on driving.

Underneath the surface of a country of endless possibility lay delusion seeping into the wells of hope like the soon-to-be poisoned groundwater from Rockwool. I thought of getting pulled over by the police and the implications for people like Denise and Rio in Cleveland. I was taking this journey hoping to feel good about America, to restore my faith in the country I was endlessly fascinated by. But maybe I was artificially whipping up hope at the expense of honesty; allowing politicians I was interviewing to tell me how wonderful they were and how well they were serving their community was perhaps not the way to best show the truth of America. For the first time since I started the journey nearly three months ago, I felt an absence of hope.

Our first stop was in Dallas (population 1.331 million). Michael and I ate noodles in the Deep Ellum neighborhood and crashed on the couch of the sister of one of our friends from Los Angeles. I felt I had lost the plot a little. Interviews weren't stacking up, despite my cold calls to legislators and city council members. We ate frozen yogurt in a nice area of town and decided to hunker down for a long drive across the state towards El Paso. On the twelve-hour trek across the desert, we drove through Marfa (population 1,831), where we stopped at the iconic roadside Prada store and took pictures with the luxury shop and desolate backdrop. The stars were miraculous, and we played Regina Spektor as we drove through the mountains.

We arrived in El Paso (population 679,813) and had breakfast at a local diner. With nothing on the agenda, we decided to drive to the border wall on the south end of the city. As we drove to the towering iron fence standing less than a hundred yards from a housing development, we needed to drive off the main road and onto a dusty street.

As we approached the border, we parked our car and walked up to the giant fence. Through the slats, we could see a small village on the other side. A young girl and two boys had noticed our arrival and ran up to the fence excitedly. The girl was maybe about five.

"Hola!" I said in broken Spanish. "My name is Ryan. Your name is what?"

The girl giggled. *"Me llamo Rosa."*

The boys didn't talk to us, they just stared. Michael approached the wall and began to converse with her in more sophisticated Spanish.

I watched through the fence as Rosa's mom walked out from her house and eyed us suspiciously.

I asked Rosa's favorite color. It was red.

As we got back into the car, I asked Michael what they had talked about. "She said she had never been to America, but she called us her 'neighbors.'"

We drove back into El Paso and to a place called the Enunciation House downtown. It was a safe haven for recent immigrants. Standing outside, we watched as four kids played soccer with a dusty rubber ball in the parking lot. We approached and said hello. There were two girls from Mexico—sisters—and one boy from Honduras. The other ran inside when we approached. We learned that this was a place that provided education and shelter to recent immigrants. As Michael asked about their individual journeys to the United States, I kicked the ball around with them. I didn't speak the language, but I could tell they were making fun of me for my lack of coordination. I was utterly charmed.

We had originally intended to go to Taos, New Mexico to meet up with Amber and Jana, but the drive seemed too taxing after our 12-hour trek to El Paso from Dallas. Instead, we decided to rent an Airbnb to afford a more leisurely pace across southern New Mexico. I opened up the app, punched our dates and "private room" into the filter, and zoomed out on the lower part of the state.

The first thing my bargain-hunting eyes saw was "$20" for a private room in a town called Truth or Consequences about two hours from El Paso. I looked up the reviews of the place—the room had a private bathroom, a fine-looking bed, and (unusually) perfect 5-star reviews across the board. The host, Keith, seemed normal enough from his picture and Michael and I were college friends of the sort where sharing a bed was inconsequential, so I booked it for that night.

Michael and I spent the day doing typical things that young men who are unaware they are about to be in mortal danger would do: we climbed over the fence into the White Sands National monument to thumb our noses at the ongoing government shutdown and drove into the mountains to the ski town of Ruidoso (population 7,791) to sample their local specialty: green chili wine, a spicy Moscato the color of pool water (and apparently a favorite of actor Mark Ruffalo). As a crepuscular pinkness lit the edge of the mountains, we decided it was time to take the hour-long drive to Truth or Consequences before dark.

Truth or Consequences (population 6,411) was originally called Hot Springs, NM, but changed their name as part of a contest to get the popular radio quiz show "Truth or Consequences" to air their 10th anniversary episode from the first town to rename themselves after the show. In 1950, Hot Springs entered and won the contest; it's unclear if a single other town was in the running.

We arrived, driving over a mountain and through the small downtown, as the navigation system directed us up a hill and into a trailer park. We drove through trailers in varying degrees of disrepair as the road turned from asphalt to gravel. We pulled onto a road at the very top of the hill and drove down the driveway of a trailer overlooking the town. It had a nice view, as the Airbnb reviews had promised.

We got our bags and rang the doorbell to the trailer. About a minute passed; we heard football on TV, rustling, and the bark of a dog. Finally, the door opened to reveal a disheveled man with a t-shirt tucked over a gut into pajama pants.

"Sorry, I was watching football," Keith mumbled, opening the door.

Inside the trailer, a fat Rottweiler wagged its tail at us.

"That's Sweetie," he said, motioning to the dog, "and that's your room," he said, pointing at a door at the end of the trailer. He squinted at us. "You both going to share the bed?"

There was a beat. Did he think…?

"We've been to five states so far…" said Michael, jumping in.

"Yeah. Just two friends on a road trip."

"We're used to it."

Keith shrugged and sat down to watch football and we went into our room. The bed was indeed small, but big enough to fit both of us. The private bathroom advertised was separated from the main room by a thin curtain. I apologized to Michael and used the bathroom. By the time I emerged our eyes met in agreement: we need to go elsewhere for a bit.

We returned to the living room to ask Keith if there were any good bars in the area.

"There's one bar," he said. "The Truth or Consequences Brewery. It's walkable from here, just down the hill."

We gathered our valuables and decided to lock them in the car, just in case. The night was cold, so as I deposited my laptop, I grabbed a jacket out of the back of the car. It was my mom's, but it seemed warm and relatively masculine even though it was kind of fuzzy. As we locked the car, we noticed that Keith had followed us out.

"Have fun at the bar," Keith said, hovering as we locked our things in my Prius.

"Yeah!" I said wildly, "who knows what we'll find tonight, truth or consequences!"

Keith smiled blandly. "More like *torture* or consequences."

Michael and I exchanged glances.

"Have a nice night," he said as he returned to the trailer.

Michael and I walked down the hill and towards the brewery, amazed at the weirdness of our situation. The city was truly small, but the downtown was well-lit in the darkness of the surrounding mountains. On the way down, I got a call from Javier, a community organizer in Albuquerque whom I was meeting the next day. When I told him where I was, he chuckled darkly.

"Wow. Don't look up David Parker Ray until you're out of there."

143

"Who's David Parker Ray?"

A pause. We turned a corner in the small downtown towards the brewery.

"He's, well, he's dead now." Javier hesitated. "So you don't have to worry about it," though something in his voice told me otherwise.

We walked into the Truth or Consequences Brewery to find three people sitting at the bar. Closest to us was who I came to know as "scary tall man with a shaved head" or "Scary Bald Man" for short. SBM was alone at the bar and immediately gave us a cockeyed appraisal on our arrival that made my skin crawl. The other two were a nice young couple at the end of the bar. Even though SBM was closest to us, we walked past the empty bar and sat down next to the couple.

After the bartender—a blue-haired woman in her sixties—took our order (a beer flight of six each) Michael and I started talking to the couple. We asked where they were from (Boston) and where they were staying. After they described their luxury yurt with a private hot spring, we unloaded our appraisal of Keith's lodging in gruesome detail. "It's at the top of the hill where the road is *gravel*. We have to *share a bed*. The bathroom has *no door!*"

I noticed that the scary bald man was listening to our conversation but thought he was simply wanting to join but too shy to do so. We continued on describing our lodging in incredulous detail as the young couple laughed and the scary bald man listened. The couple told us all about their travels through the southwest and the local hot springs in the downtown that they had gone to and highly suggested we visit the next morning.

Suddenly, I got a FaceTime call from Amber. I finished up one of the beer flights and picked up, walking back towards the bathroom area and chatting loudly. As we FaceTimed, I noticed the scary bald man coming back towards the bathroom. I moved out of the way as he walked past, but as he approached me, his scary bald face leaned in towards me, leered, and yelled "FAGGOT!" into my phone.

I was more confused than offended. Was he talking to me? My friend on FaceTime? Was it some weird attempt at a joke? I asked Amber if she had heard the slur. She had, and we decided to laugh it off.

After my conversation, I returned to my seat. SBM had not returned but was visible through the front window smoking by a gray pickup truck parked outside. I quickly picked up another glass from my beer flight and told my companions about the bizarre thing that had just happened. They responded immediately by whipping around to look at SBM out the window, who—naturally—was staring back at us, grinning a crooked grin.

We were suddenly interrupted by the blue-haired bartender. "The eclipse is 75% done! You guys gotta go out and watch it!"

Another detail of the evening was that it was the night of the "Super Blood Moon" eclipse. We had forgotten that it was occurring until her blue-haired reminder. Wanting to see the eclipse, but hesitating to go out by SBM, one of our Boston friends had an easy fix: "Is there any way we can watch from behind the bar for less light pollution?"

The bartender gave us permission to use the back door, so Michael and I left our beer flights unattended and followed our friends out back to the parking lot as the bartender began prepping to close the bar.

Weirdly, the eclipse wasn't even 15 minutes from starting when we went out, not 75% complete as the bartender had indicated. We stood outside waiting and finally watched in amazement as the moon went from its usual glow to a dull red sphere in the sky, taking away the light from the already dark parking lot. After the eclipse, our fancy new friends decided to go back to their yurt, so we bid them well and went around the front of the building and back into the brewery.

Scary Bald Man was back at the bar. We walked towards our

seats and as we passed, he looked at us with that unsettling smile and said, "you guys feeling alright?"

My default mode is friendly, so I automatically responded "Yeah, fine, just saw the eclipse!" and hurried back to my seat to work on my remaining three beers. Michael now seemed uneasy, as though that passing exchange had confirmed my story.

"Are you sure you're okay being here right now?"

For all the virtues of compromise I espoused on this trip, there are two principles I will not compromise. First, I will never leave a beer unfinished. Second, I will never let anyone intimidate me into doing something I don't want to do (like leaving a beer unfinished). So I said no, and started downing my remaining drinks. Michael hesitantly followed suit, shooting glances over to SBM who we now noticed was no longer alone.

Scary Bald Man was joined now by Short Brunette Man, conveniently both acronym-ed SBM (and incidentally the same acronym as Super Blood Moon). They were cackling about how ShortBM had recently been left by a woman, but he had stolen her car. I ignored them and continued drinking, until I went to drink my final beer glass, placed directly between Michael and me.

"Don't drink that!" Michael said suddenly.

I paused. "Why not?"

"I just... I'm getting bad juju right now." He counted his glasses. "You've already finished all of yours. And I have all of mine." He pointed to the full beer. "So this is extra."

I looked at Michael's worried face and over at the two men, who were watching us.

I compromised my integrity; I didn't drink the additional beer.

Eventually, the two men got up and left the bar, but lingered outside by the gray truck. I didn't want to admit to myself that it seemed like they were waiting for us, but it did. In the meantime, we made small talk with the bartender as she prepared the bar for closing before I finally decided to ask about SBM.

"Do you know that bald guy at the end of the bar at all?"

The blue-haired woman nodded. "He buys kegs from us some-times. Why?"

"He said something kind of weird to me."

"A slur," added Michael.

"*Really?*" she said with a theatrical gesture of surprise. "That doesn't sound like him at all."

We glanced outside. SBM and SBM and the truck were both gone.

"Well!" said the bartender. "It's closing time. Here are your checks!"

We paid, surprised by how quickly the bartender seemed to want us out of the brewery. As she turned off the lights, we walked out of the bar and heard the lock click behind us. We looked into the deserted, well-lit street. We breathed a sigh of relief, smiled at each other nervously, and started walking back towards Keith's.

Only three steps off the sidewalk, we saw it: a gray pickup truck hurtling down the parallel street towards our Airbnb.

Michael shook his head. "We gotta hide," and darted onto someone's front porch. I didn't want anyone else involved, so I pulled him off, pointing out that he was just as visible there as from the street.

"Let's keep walking," I said, and I soldiered on towards the hill up to Keith's.

The gray pickup truck rounded the corner ahead and drove straight towards me.

I froze as the truck bounded down the street. It drove, head-lights momentarily blinding me and, when it reached me, turned on the perpendicular street and stopped. I watched: as I had feared, SBM and SBM both got out of the car. SBM emerged from the passenger seat got into the driver's seat and the other for some reason got into the back seat. I didn't wait to find out why. I started running towards the less-illuminated trailer park on the hill, hoping Michael would follow suit. The next thing I knew, as I sprinted, I was cut off by the gray truck, which was barreling up the road to the top of the trailer park. Unsure if it saw me, I hid in the bushes waiting for Michael to catch up. When I finally heard footsteps, I tensed, fearing the worst.

It was Michael. He looked just as panic-stricken as I imagined I did.

"Let's run."

Together, we ran through the trailer park, stopping to hide in the shadows behind trailers when we heard vehicles, but eventually finding our way back to the "safety" of Keith's home.

Once inside, we turned to each other.

"Are we freaking out right now?"

"Maybe a little?"

"Should we not stay here tonight?"

Our hearts were still racing.

"Do you think…"

"Keith?"

"Is that crazy?"

"He tipped them off?"

"No, we have to be reasonable… the door locks to our room."

"But he has a key!"

In the end, we decided that being outside or driving a car in a remote area was riskier than our Airbnb host being a potential accomplice. We both slept with one eye open and woke up at dawn to make our way down to the hot springs tourist destination and safety. We spent a luxurious morning with a Japanese couple in a natural hot tub, talking about America's individualism versus Japan's social cohesion, and by the time we got out of the water, we had cleansed ourselves of all memories of SBM, SBM, and Keith. Until I checked my phone and found that I had a voicemail.

Hey Ryan, this is Keith. Didn't see you this morning just wanted to… just make sure you and your friend got out okay. Okay.

Never in my five years using Airbnb had I ever received a call from a host and was not aware how my number was available to him. I dashed off a quick "thank you!!!!" text to Keith and we got to the car, ready to put distance between us and Truth or Consequences.

In the car, I got a notification on my phone. I had an Airbnb message from Keith.

Ryan, hope you and your friend had a nice stay. You said you are writing a book about your travels through the 50 states / bars. Google the name David Parker Ray.

I read it to Michael. We both agreed. We would not look up David Parker Ray until we were a hundred miles out of Truth or Consequences.

On the way out of town, we passed a sign for a state park called Elephant Butte. For some reason, I remembered reading something about it somewhere. I decided to pull into the park to have a quick look around.

It was stunning. The quintessential plateaued rocks of the Southwest stretched over the horizon around a deep blue lake. We drove and admired the vast space as slowly the road turned from asphalt to gravel, gravel to sand…

"Shit, we're on the beach," I realized.

"Just keep driving fast," Michael told me. "There's another Prius over there by the water."

"I think we should go back, the sand looks really deep."

"Just keep going fast."

I kept driving across the beach towards the gravel road on the other side, but sure enough, Belinda got mired in the sand, stalled, and stopped moving altogether.

I got out of the car and surveyed the situation. We tried to remain calm. I went around the back of the car and tried to push as Michael drove and found that Belinda wouldn't budge. We were stuck in Truth or Consequences.

I screamed into the void.

"We can get out!" said Michael, but I knew he didn't believe it.

We stood around, trying to push and drive, but it was no use.

"We could call a tow truck?" began Michael.

"A *tow truck*?" I said wildly. "Who do you think is going to be driving that truck, Michael?"

"Scary Bald Man," Michael said, eyes on the sandy ground.

"That's right! With our luck in this town, Scary Bald Man is going to show up, and they'll find our bodies buried here next spring!" But I noticed that Michael wasn't looking at me anymore. He was gazing towards the horizon. I turned around. Like something out of a weird Toyota commercial, a gold Prius was gliding across the beach towards our own stranded Prius. My mouth was agape at this real-life *deus ex machina* as two young men emerged with a shovel and asked if we needed help. I could barely speak.

Feeling as if I were in a dream, I got into the driver's seat and gave my all to the gas pedal as Michael and the two angels pushed the car. I turned the wheel vigorously to both sides, and miraculously, the car sped forward across the beach and towards freedom.

I heard them shouting, "Keep going! Keep going!" as I drove towards the road. I did as I was told. Finally on solid gravel, I stopped the car and looked back. Michael was running towards me grinning and the golden Prius was driving away. Wherever those guys are now, I hope they've won the lottery.

Finally, with Michael in the car, we drove away on the solid, reliable asphalt highway away from Truth or Consequences and Elephant Butte State Park. We didn't speak. Only when we were 45 miles from Albuquerque did I turn to Michael.

"Tell me about David Parker Ray."

Michael nodded and did some research on his phone. I waited for him to say something.

"Michael?"

He turned to me. "It's good we got out of there."

We discovered a few things about David Parker Ray. He was arrested in 2001 for drugging, kidnapping, raping, torturing, and murdering over 60 people. DPR was known as the "Toy-Box Killer" because he did his torturing in a trailer. This trailer happened to be located in Elephant Butte. DPR had a few specific quirks, such as the interesting fact that he liked to have mirrors in his trailer so his victims could see themselves being tortured. DPR's daughter, Glenda Jean, was his accomplice: she would drug people's beers so her father could kidnap them.

My jaw dropped at this.

Despite being an accomplice to a serial killer, Glenda Jean only served two and half years in prison. DPR allegedly had other accomplices: girlfriends, law enforcement, and, most relevantly, local bartenders. Many of these people were not caught or got off on plea deals. Even though DPR died in 2002, many of his accomplices are at large today. Many still live in Truth or Consequences.

The final fact was the one that chilled us the most. We read that the bodies of David Parker Ray's victims were disposed of in an abandoned mine next to a lake in a little place called Elephant Butte State Park, less than a half mile from where our Prius was marooned.

I wish I could say I remember much of the rest of New Mexico. In Albuquerque (population 559,374), we talked to a community organizer, Javier, who worked with rural New Mexicans to fight for a living wage. We visited the First Nations Health Clinic, which provides every service under the sun from health care, job training, housing, and legal services. We visited the Mayor's Office and talked about Albuquerque's role in decentralizing the entertainment industry with their new Netflix headquarters. We stayed in a loft in a solar-powered home with a green architect. We met a woman who helped commit doctor-assisted suicides. But still, it all paled in comparison to what we had experienced in Truth or Consequences.

Something in my gut told me something was off all along, but it didn't compute. Why did SBM want to come after us? I was just a normal dude wearing his mother's fuzzy coat minding his own business with his male companion; he had no reason to think anything else. I had encountered the danger that marginalized groups experienced, danger that those with privilege sometimes discount. I realized that fear was learned from malice at the hands of people like Scary Bald Man. It wasn't logical; our fear was their pleasure. As much as I want to believe all Americans are good—and I believe most are—I had my nose pressed up against a simple fact, a fact that Joe Towns Jr. had reminded me of during our interview in Nashville: evil people are still abound.

THE WEST

STILL SHAKEN from our experience in Truth or Consequences, Michael and I drove north into Colorado. While the danger from serial killers had seemingly subsided, there was a nasty snowstorm on our way into Denver, prompting us to leave the city quickly in favor of Longmont (population 94,445), just outside of Boulder. We were staying in the guest house of the parents of a college friend— Janet and Pete were excellent hosts and excellent chefs. After settling in, they treated us to individual roast chickens, allowing us to regale the story of how we had almost been murdered. The next day, Janet took us to see some of her volunteer work on the outskirts of town: an English tutoring session in the home of recent immigrants. As Janet taught the English words for items at the grocery store to a 40-year-old woman from Honduras, I watched as the woman's young daughter stood in the doorway and listened.

The next day, Michael and I decided that, in order to understand the Colorado state of mind, we should go and sample legalized weed. We were in a comfortable guest house on a snowy day, and it seemed like a cozy way to spend a Colorado evening after another fabulous dinner from Janet and Pete. My own state of mind had become increasingly susceptible to paranoia due to recent events, and—after sampling the two gummies recommended to us—the crushing weight of everything I had experienced came crashing down. The worries about the financial aspect of the trip began to compound with the terror we had just experienced in New Mexico and the dark underbelly of the country I had discovered in Oklahoma. As we struggled to set up the Roku on the guest house TV, I started reeling. Michael went into the bedroom, seeming to be similarly traumatized from our Truth or Consequences adventure, leaving me alone on the couch. That night, high and spiraling, I wrote this message to myself:

"The arrogance of what I've set out to do truly astounds me. The fact that I could think I could ever try to wade into the battles of our long-held divisions absolutely terrifies me. BUT. I know I can understand and synthesize people instead of putting them into little boxes. That's all I've got."

I woke up the next day a little horrified at my freakout. I looked into my journal and rolled my eyes at my own state of mind.

Michael emerged from the bedroom, looking sheepish, his strawberry blonde hair ruffled. "Wasn't indica supposed to be relaxing? In da couch?"

"I want my money back."

As we went to go say goodbye to Janet and Peter, their small smirks over the morning paper conveyed that they may have suspected exactly what we were doing the night before.

Next, Michael and I went to visit my cousin in Colorado Springs (population 464,871). Annie was a senior at Colorado College, and I always found her to have a grounded and wise presence despite her being younger than me. We sat in her college house just off campus as her roommates trickled in. Eventually, Michael and I were holding court, once again telling the story of our daring escape from Truth or Consequences. One of Annie's roommates returned with her boyfriend, Ethan, who was a sophomore in the Air Force. As we started talking, I realized I hadn't yet spoken to anyone in the military, so I pulled out my recording device and started an interview.

"What do you like about the Air Force?"

Ethan, tall and lanky, cracked a beer we had brought from an Oklahoma City brewery. "We feel like as a population, as a group of people, we are a lot closer than the regular student body. We really have each other's back. I may not know another cadet, but I can count on them. That's really nice. We call the whole thing a fraternity. I grew up in a small town in Texas. I was used to hanging out with one or two groups of people. And I came here, and it rocked my world, being outside of my little bubble of a town. It's a very diverse group of people."

"I was talking to someone the other day about a mandatory year of service," I said, thinking of my time visiting with a group of AmeriCorps students at High Point. "Of course, this doesn't necessarily mean it has to be military service, it can be volunteering for AmeriCorps." I said. "Do you think something like that would bring the country together?"

Ethan nodded vigorously. "There's something about getting different groups of people together from different parts of the country, different parts of the world that leads to more understanding. On the surface, you seem really different, but when you start talking you all have a common goal. To serve your country. Doesn't matter what a person sitting across from you looks like, or where they're from. And that really squashes a lot of problems, at least in the military."

Driving across the border into Wyoming, the snow was blowing wildly. I was thinking about the lack of social cohesion in America and how we seemed to lack a common purpose. I wished we had another public forum besides the military to help people understand and befriend people from around the country, like I had been able to over the past three months.

I felt trepidation as I drove towards Wyoming, one of the most unknown states for me personally. Michael and I were on our way to Cheyenne (population 63,607) for a meeting with one of the state senators. I wasn't sure what to expect, but Senator Bill Landon, a Republican from Natrona County, was an incredibly generous host. He invited me and Michael onto the floor of the legislature and formally recognized each of us, explaining the purpose of the trip and prompting the entire legislature to erupt in applause. Nowhere in the United States had I received such a welcome. It wasn't the reason I came to love Wyoming, but it certainly didn't hurt.

After our visit with the Wyoming House of Representatives, we drove to Laramie (population 32,381) to visit a friend from high school, Molly. The stories of Matthew Shepard's 1998 murder in Laramie loomed large in my head as we drove past the Wal-Mart and into the quaint center of the Wyoming college town. We were now visiting the home of the most famous anti-gay crime in history where Matthew Shepard, a 21-year-old University of Wyoming student, was beaten and robbed by two young men after meeting him at a bar. They took Matthew out past the Wal-Mart, tied him to a fence, tortured him, and left him to die in the cold. The outrage that followed Matthew Shepard's death drew global attention and trickled its way into the national psyche. I first learned about his death while I was in high school, reckoning with my own future.

We arrived at Molly's house on the outskirts of campus, an immaculately decorated two-room guest house. When I saw her—bright green eyes, blonde wavy hair, stylish outfit—she could've been the same Molly I knew in high school, part of a pack of girls who were decidedly the prettiest and most popular, but Molly had an independent streak. As she welcomed us in, cracking jokes about ending up in Wyoming for grad school, I sensed that same hint of the mischievousness I had always loved about her. I considered us kindred spirits then; seeing as she too was doing a master's in creative writing here at the University of Wyoming, I felt a rush of affection for Molly.

As Molly toured us around Laramie, I tried to focus on the town, but I found myself reminiscing about my final months of high school. It was April of my senior year and the decision to stay closeted in high school was expiring. Buoyed by my acceptance to Northwestern and my excitement to finally go off and live authentically in Evanston, the stakes of high school melted away. As college acceptance season began to wind down, the season of prom invitations commenced. The rumor mill of who was hoping to be asked by whom was in full swing, and—while I was privately dreaming of the impossibility of bringing a secret boyfriend—I was approached with a surprising piece of news: Molly wanted to go to prom with me. We were friendly but not necessarily friends; I had always considered her a few social echelons above me in the high school hierarchy. Once I confirmed from various sources that this was true, I invited Molly to a party at my house to scope out the situation; when she showed up I found her surprisingly interested, flirtatious even, and I wondered if she had sensed something approachable, non-threatening in me that told her that—while I probably wouldn't be the one to seal the deal with her on prom night—I wouldn't slip anything in her drink either. I asked her to prom in Anatomy class via a doctored video about osteoporosis I had spliced to include an actor friend who broke the fourth wall and asked her to go to prom with me, before "You Make My Dreams Come True" by Hall & Oates started playing over a series of sobering facts about female skeletons. I pulled out a bouquet of flowers and asked if she wanted to go to prom with me. Molly accepted. So began our promship.

Molly and I started to hang out after school: I remember sitting at the Spring Garden Diner a few blocks from my high school, eating breakfast for dinner and gossiping about people in our class. It was exciting, making a new friend at the end of high school. That Saturday night, after watching *Garden State* at my house, I showed Molly to the door. Though I had expected nothing but platonic feelings towards her, there was a surprising charge between us, and something was telling me that Molly wasn't totally opposed to ending the night with something more than a friendly hug. I thought better of it, instead deciding to walk her to the red VW parked in the driveway. We said goodbye, and I rushed back into the house, where my parents were waiting.

"We like Molly," they said.

"Yeah, me too." I replied. The normalcy of all of this was bizarre to me, like I had slipped into another boy's apple pie American life.

"Ask her if she'd like to go to dinner with us before you take her to prom, my treat," my dad said.

I felt my pocket buzz. I looked down to see a call from Molly.

"Hello?"

"Ry? I got lost. I'm back in your driveway," Molly said with an embarrassed laugh.

I immediately felt guilty. It was 2010, before Google Maps, and I assumed I hadn't given her proper instructions. I ran outside to where she sat in her car, window open, looking sheepish.

"Hey!" I said, bounding over. "I'm so sorry, my neighborhood is really confusing…"

"It's okay," she said, a smile around the corners of her mouth.

"You just… take a right," I said, pausing to picture the route in my head, "then go all the way to Riverside Road, and then… um…"

I noticed that she really didn't seem to be listening.

"Sorry, I'm really bad at explaining directions."

"No, no… I think I got it now," she said, smiling.

"Are you sure?"

"Yeah. I definitely have it now."

There was a pause.

"Oh! My parents asked if you wanted to get dinner next weekend. Their treat, obviously…"

"I'd like that."

Another silence. I felt the same electric anticipation crackling unexpectedly in the air.

"Well, I'm gonna get home."

"I'm glad to see you again."

I noticed her lip gloss glinting in the light.

"Drive careful," I said.

"I will," she replied.

"K… well…"

"Bye."

"Bye."

And as though I had suddenly overtaken a character in *Dawson's Creek*, I leaned down and kissed the girl who was out of my league, feeling the surprising sensation not only of the softness of her lips, but of the fact that this moment of intimacy was in no way doomed to be a secret.

I opened my eyes to see Molly looking pleased that her ploy had worked. I stood up, wonderfully surprised at my own daring.

"Drive safe, Molly," I said, grinning.

"Text you when I'm home," she said, red-nailed hands changing the gears on her stick shift.

The following weeks were borrowed from someone else's life. Everything about my romantic history up to this point had been an act of defiance, and this chapter felt effortless and easy. The dinner with my parents and Molly was enjoyable, fun even, and I found myself genuinely looking forward to spending time with her after school or on the weekends. Even though I was still clumsy with girls, I found that skills I had acquired weren't totally irrelevant with Molly. I wondered how this unexpected door had opened and if this was my one shot to cast away the difficult life my father had foreshadowed for me and focus simply on being happy with a girl. I hated to admit it to myself, but the approval from my parents, my friends, even my brother, was intoxicating. Feeling the entirety of their approval for the first time made me realize I had never experienced its full potency, as though I was finally witnessing the majesty of a full moon after years of crescents. It felt so easy, doing what I was supposed to. And this All-American version of myself, finally getting the approval I felt I deserved, is something I often think back to, no matter how brief it was. The new effortlessness was foreign but thrilling; an intoxicating respite from trying to prove something, to make up for something.

I was trying to keep my nostalgia at bay, but it wasn't easy; I hadn't seen Molly in nearly five years. Michael, Molly, and I ate downtown Laramie that evening and then decided to go bar hopping. I told very little of this backstory to Michael as we went from a bar lined with deer antlers to one where karaoke was in full swing. I noticed Michael and Molly joking around, and I tried to ignore the slight echo of jealousy. The Library Sports Grille & Brewery was full of people. I got up and sang "Faith" by George Michael, my go-to karaoke song. When I was done, a woman came over and began telling me how she was a "GILF" (like a MILF, but for a grandma) before she was promptly kicked out of the establishment for drunken behavior. Molly had been watching my exchange with the GILF—she walked over to me and we started talking about old times and her adjustment to Laramie. She looked around the bar, where someone had just started belting the chorus of "The Middle" by Jimmy Eat World.

I looked at two male college students at the bar and thought of Matthew Shepard. Matthew Shepard's murder was familiar to any theatre person through the ubiquitous performances of *The Laramie Project* done all across the country, detailing the effects of his murder on Laramie. Was it a bar like this where he met the men who would lead him to his death? I thought of myself walking into the bar in Truth or Consequences, him walking into a bar like this one. As I traveled, I could choose just how much of my identity to share with those I met. It was called "code-switching," something that certain members of the LGBTQ community can do to "blend in." I had the privilege of doing this often on the trip for my convenience (luckily no one had seen me throw a football thus far on the trip).

As I spoke to Molly, I realized that I've never been able to tell her the truth. During my junior year of college, while I was nine months into dating my first serious boyfriend, we met up in downtown Rockford during my spring break. What started out as a cordial catching up at a local pub turned into a bar crawl and then into something that almost felt like a date again, after all these years. And in the dark moments when I stumbled through relationships, encountering the fickleness in my crushes and in myself, or when I saw gay couples over the age of 50 dealing with discrimination, a small shameful part of me always decided that Molly would be there, on the back burner for me, the same way I had been for her.

Molly met up with a boy she'd been seeing at the Ruffed Up Duck Saloon, and Michael and I started talking to some locals about Wyoming. When I told the two older women where we had come from and asked about Matthew Shepard, they told me that they in Laramie were not anti-gay at all. "Matthew Shepard, it was all about drugs. I hope you know that. We're not like that here."

Outside of the Ruffed Up Duck Saloon, Molly and her suitor parted. We walked back to Molly's place and through the downtown, passing college kids in cowboy hats horsing around. As Michael and Molly chatted ahead of me, I was very aware of where I was, in the town where Matthew Shepard was attacked, but also where I was in my life. The truth I had hidden from Molly made me think of my mental desire to create an off-ramp. My time with her in high school was significant, not because it was a high school fling that I was still hung up on, but because it represented the fleeting chance that maybe I could believe "it was all just a phase," a common refrain LGBTQ people hear. When I was living in New York, I struggled to find someone to settle down with. It was due to transient nature of the city, but I was also to blame. My high standards meant that I rarely found someone I could see a future with, and when I did, the timing was never right. Maybe I was moving somewhere else, maybe they weren't in a place to get serious. I didn't admit to myself that I had a mental off-ramp, but I was suddenly faced with the fact that when I arrived at Oxford, I specifically kept my sexuality vague. Maybe I would meet my British Molly there. Maybe that was the only way for me to find someone.

I thought of what I had gone through with Paul. Was there a part of me coming here that thought what I experienced in Tennessee was all just a preamble to something else, that Molly would offer clarity? Was I faced with a binary choice: a man who couldn't commit to me or a woman from whom I would have to hide a part of myself? That night, I understood for the first time that Molly represented an exit ramp since I was eighteen; exit ramps weren't going to be the answer to my problems. I had followed these off-ramps—girls I met over the past years—to disastrous consequences. I was attracted by the simplicity, but once I realized another human being was involved I saw I was making a terrible mistake. As we arrived back at Molly's house, I watched as she made up a pull-out couch for Michael and me. It was time to close those off-ramps for good and follow the road I was on.

We went to sleep extremely late and had to be up early for our drive to Casper. As we drove on the narrow-one lane road north, a squall shook Belinda, the wind blowing gusts of snow in front of the windshield. As Michael slept in the passenger's seat, I gripped the wheel for dear life as I sped towards Casper (population 58,446).

We were staying with Sloan, a local news anchor and another friend from high school. We arrived at Sloan's apartment in the small city. Sloan and I had met during my year at a Canadian boarding school. Lanky, affable, and blond, Sloan looked like the quintessential newscaster from the 1950s. He hailed from Seattle but had moved to Casper for work and had become completely enchanted with it. He was so enthralled with where he had been stationed—as newscasters, like the military, have very little agency over where they live starting out—that he reached out to me directly when he heard about my trip and implored me to come to Casper. I was exhausted as Sloan drove us into town, but I was instantly animated by the fascinating interviews that he had curated.

First, Sloan took Michael and me to Backwards Distillery and introduced me to the owner, Amber, who had returned to Casper and started the distillery with her wife. Over a craft cocktail made with their homemade gin, I talked to Amber about her decision to come home to Wyoming to build a business and a life.

"It's really exciting to be in Casper now. But after starting the business, these last three or four years we have a critical mass of cool people that are doing cool things. And it's to the point where there's enough of that happening that you see a noticeable change in the town. Just one person doing something cool is not really enough to move the needle in terms of the overall vibe of the place. It's a cool time to be here, because you've got the opportunity to participate in it, versus moving into a place that's ready-made. It's way more exciting to be in a place where you see potential and you also feel like you can influence that, and the people around you are influencing it too."

"Do you feel like being a progressive person in Casper has made it better?"

"I can't take all the credit for that, certainly. But I think that's so. Distilleries and breweries become a gathering point, people are emotionally attached to them. By extension, people get emotionally attached to the people involved in that. And I think we've worked really hard to be a positive force in the community so that people would attach positive feelings to us and our business. People know who I am in the community; I've gotten involved beyond the business as well. Naturally, you know, my more progressive sort of viewpoint comes along with me, and I think that's what you need. Otherwise you're ending up in this sort of echo chamber. I mean, I'm not saying it's getting more progressive politically necessarily, but certainly I would feel more comfortable coming here now… as myself… than I would have four years ago."

She sighed.

"My wife made Pride into a four-day extravaganza. It was on MTV. People here, I don't think, understand the impact of Matthew Shepard in terms of what people *think* about us nationally and internationally. We have to make the statement because if we don't make the statement, we haven't done anything to give people any reason to believe that it's not normal or not the usual. Because for all they know, it is."

I didn't know it at the time, but Amber would be elected to the city council of Casper only years later, proving her words prescient.

Next, Sloan took Michael and me downtown to meet with the mayor of Casper, Charlie Powell. Walking into a coffee shop, we found a man in a crisp shirt and gray hair, a contrast to the cowboy hat-wearing men I had seen walking outside of the shop. As we sat down and ordered coffee, Mayor Powell talked to us about the passage of a controversial nondiscrimination clause to protect LGBTQ people in Casper, a law that Amber had referenced.

"A year ago we passed a nondiscrimination resolution that was very controversial in our little town because this is a very conservative environment. But we were just talking about the Shepard murder. That was 20 years ago. And it seems to me that has played a factor in how people view Wyoming. And we've even heard stories where people had an opportunity to move to Wyoming and they were told by their friends, if they were gay, 'don't go there, you could get shot. They hate gay people there.' And it's not true. It's an image challenge that we have," said Powell over the hiss of an espresso maker. "It's not so much about inviting all the gay and lesbian people into Wyoming or Casper, although they're welcome. Everybody's welcome if they've got something to contribute. But it's about a message to an entire generation that thinks that having a problem with people because of their sexual orientation is goofy. And why would you want to be in a place where people think that way? And I think if they were to pass the statute in the state, it would at least cause some people to take a second look and say, 'Well, maybe I was wrong about that.'"

From the coffee shop, Sloan took us to the iconic Casper staple Lou Taubert Ranch Outfitters, a sprawling store full of cowboy hats.

"I buy everyone who comes to visit me a cowboy hat," said Sloan, looking at the shelves of hats. "Time for you to get yours."

I spent nearly an hour trying on hats. I was like a kid in a candy store, picking out an item that felt as novel to me as a vestment from a foreign culture. I finally found a gray-brown Stetson hat that looked a little large for my head, but I was assured by the shopkeeper that it was the style in Casper. Who was I to argue?

As we left the store, it was twilight in the little city. As I gazed out over the snow-covered mountains, glowing gold in the dying light, I looked over at Michael, who grinned back at me; we were totally enchanted.

That night, Sloan took us out dancing at a bar to show off our new hats. At the Beacon Club—a barn-like bar covered in neon signs—I watched as locals stopped him to chat, recognizing him from the news, until finally a woman approached and asked him to dance. He went out on the dance floor, literally spinning and twirling the woman as a live band played. As I looked around the bar, I felt I had stumbled upon a culture that was singularly unique and special here in Casper.

The woman breathlessly came back to our table. Her name was Cathy, and she insisted we had to come visit her ranch. Sloan assured us it was not an empty offer, and so the next day we went to visit her home. We met her husband, whom she described as a cowboy, and talked about her journey from growing up in Milwaukee and moving to Wyoming to become, as she branded herself, a "Prairie Wife in Heels." She proudly showed us the elk in the freezer that her thirteen-year-old son had hunted ("it will feed us for a year!") and took us outside to ride her horses. The zest she had for her life, her family, her neighbors was infectious.

"I love it here. It's like the way they described the 1950s," Cathy told me as she fed her chickens. "Leaving your doors unlocked, letting your kids grow into themselves running free." She smiled, looking across the mountainous landscape, the wind whipping her hair. "It's a special place."

Sloan took Michael and me to the home of former Governor Mike Sullivan, a Democrat who held statewide office in Wyoming. As we drove onto the highway, I saw a large mural painted onto the side of a barn. "Freedom ends where regulation begins."

The final day in Casper, Sloan was able to have me as a guest on his local news show, "Report To Wyoming" to talk about my travels. As I sat in the middle of a panel of local Wyoming talking heads, they asked me what I had learned so far on the trip.

"How do we get young people like you to come to places like Wyoming?" one panelist asked me.

The realization that had been developing for so long finally had a moment to be articulated. I found myself thinking of the words of my first interview in Ohio with Gambier mayor Kachen Kimmel. "Young people need to get brave and move away from the coasts. If you're young and have talent, you need to go to places where you can have impact."

The men beside me nodded fervently. I kept talking, not sure if I should look at the camera or not.

"We need to start volunteering in our communities." I said, excited to finally be able to explain what I had been learning. "We need to stand up and fight and actually do something about the problems we complain about. If you're young and you have passion, we should go to places where we can actually be a part of shaping a community," I said, thinking of what Amber had told me. I rattled off statistics and anecdotes from the places I had visited, feeling that there was no better place than Wyoming to test drive the message.

As we left the studio, I said goodbye to Sloan.

"You seriously gave me one of the best gifts on the trip," I said, shaking his hand. "And I don't just mean the hat. The way you curated this whole thing… it really made me fall in love with the city."

Sloan winked. "All by design."

As Michael and I got in the car, we both looked at each other, silently asking the same question: "Are we both moving to Casper, Wyoming?"

I thought of Amber's ability to live in Casper with her wife. Did this mean it would be possible for me too?

From Wyoming, Michael and I drove up to Victor, Idaho (population 1,928). We were staying with my Aunt Alice and Uncle Bill, who lived in a beautiful cabin in the mountains. Inside, the house was unbelievably cozy, with a wood stove in the living room and a staircase leading up to the bedrooms. Aunt Alice frequently returned to the kitchen, where a cappuccino maker was constantly whirring as she shuttled warm mugs into our hands. The first night we were in town, there had been fresh snow, so Uncle Bill wanted to take us to experience one of his favorite winter adventures. He was coy about what exactly we were about to do as he fit Michael and I with helmets and headlamps.

"What are these for?"

"We're… night sledding."

We grabbed the wooden sleds, which I noticed had levers to steer on the left and right sides. Uncle Bill's friend Jasper picked us up in a van and drove to the top of the mountain, where Jasper would be driving behind us "in case you crash." As we drove up in the van, I didn't realize quite how high we were going.

"Uncle Bill?" I asked. "What *does* happen if we crash?"

Uncle Bill smiled and shrugged. "Try not to crash."

On the top of the mountain, we got into position in the middle of an icy road as we held the brakes down on our sleds.

Uncle Bill walked over and looked down the mountain.

"So remember to lean a little bit as you go around curves," he said, pointing down at the icy road. "And there's a large snowbank on the other side of the road most of the way, so as long as you crash into that you should be good.

"Most of the way?"

Uncle Bill shrugged. "You're on an adventure. Lean into it."

I let go. The brakes unstuck from the ice as I started sliding down the frozen road. The blades on the sled held tight to the ground as I pressed down on the lever and leaned into a turn. This was some of the most fun I had had on the trip so far: feeling the cold wind whip my face as I slid towards the base of the mountain, I estimated I must've been going nearly 30 mph. I heard Michael whoop from behind me, and I let out a yell back.

Then I crashed into a snow drift.

But I pulled myself out, dusted myself off, and continued to ice luge down the sleepy mountain road. Idaho presented me with true exhilaration and the warmth of reconnecting with my family. Though Aunt Alice and Uncle Bill took me to an informative round table of local government officials the next day, the best part about the state was the joy of having an excuse to see the beauty in the place my family had chosen to live. I could tell they were proud of how much Michael and I palpably loved Victor, Idaho, a place my family hadn't visited often enough. When I told them I wished I could build a life like theirs somewhere, I meant it.

Driving south to Utah, we stayed in Salt Lake City (population 197,756) for an evening with friends of Mark, who was my fraternity chapter advisor at Northwestern. Mark was a serious, strait-laced man in his 60s from Utah, who always intimidated me when I was a pledge. I remember in my final interview before joining the fraternity, I was terrified that Mark might know that I was different from the other pledges in my class.

My sophomore year, I had to do something awkward. I had to stand in front of the chapter because I wanted to ask permission from the group to bring my boyfriend to our Spring Formal. As far as I knew, this would be a first at my fraternity, and I didn't want to do something that would make another brother so uncomfortable that it would ruin their night. Unfortunately, the night I decided to do so, Mark was in attendance, announcing some official Sigma Chi business. I didn't have a choice but to ask if I could bring my boyfriend to the formal in front of Mark.

The request was phrased as a question with an addendum that if anyone had an issue to let me know. It was met with applause, but when I stole a look at Mark's face, it was inscrutable.

Later that night, I got a call from an unknown number.

"Ryan? It's Mark."

My heart stopped.

"I just wanted to say that was a real act of courage, what you did tonight." He cleared his throat gruffly.

"Thank you, Mark," I replied.

"And... well, I haven't told anyone in the house this, but... me and my partner Peter have been together going on thirty years now..."

I didn't understand what I was hearing.

"And the way you spoke tonight made me think maybe it doesn't need to be such a secret after all," Mark said. "Times are changing."

Mark and Peter became close friends and mentors, showing up to my performances at Northwestern and taking me out to lunches after I graduated. I never realized how connected they were to the LGBTQ community in Utah, but as we slept in the converted garage of an older lesbian couple, I felt I got to see some of Mark's roots, even as he was still living in Evanston.

The first night in Salt Lake City I was meeting with an old friend of mine from a former job. Tracey was a volunteer at the Salt Lake City Police Department when we met. I was working as an associate producer on "Cold Justice: Sex Crimes." My job was to find unsolved cold cases and provide resources for them to be solved on a documentary TV episode. I had met Tracey through cold calling police departments, and our friendship had blossomed from talking about untested rape kits over the phone to sending each other recipes via email. This would be my first time meeting her in person. We met at the Red Iguana, a Mexican restaurant that specialized in various molés. She was a smiling woman with long blonde hair, and I instantly recognized her voice.

Over a multicolored molé plate, we reminisced about the work we were able to accomplish together on the show.

"Why did you leave?"

"I went to work for the Hillary Clinton campaign."

I watched as she shifted uncomfortably in her seat. "Oh! Good for you."

"But there's *plenty* I can criticize," I said, launching into the story of the scorching Florida rally and the overflow section.

The conversation thawed quite a bit after that. She even invited me to her houseboat on Lake Powell.

The next day, Michael and I toured a factory sponsored by the Church of the Latter-Day Saints, where they showed us how they made their own products to distribute free of charge. We wanted to get down to Bryce Canyon at a decent hour, so we started driving early, also because we wanted to ensure we didn't arrive too late at the home of our next host in Arizona.

The natural beauty of southern Utah was breathtaking. I was getting nostalgic as I realized this would be my last state with Michael. I was thinking of how so many of my most important relationships were marked by long road trips: road trips with my parents, road trips with my exes, road trips with friends whom I'd drifted from. I thought of how life on the road allowed people to see an authentic picture of one another. At my worst, I knew I could be sullen, argumentative, mistrustful, and I have always feared someone seeing those parts of me. I looked over at Michael, sleeping in the passenger seat, and thought how lucky I was to have a friend.

· · ·

We arrived so late in Scottsdale (population 250,602), it was embarrassing. It was nearly midnight when we arrived at Vince's front door. Vince was a friend of one of my uncles and we were staying in his winter condo. Hoping to brighten the mood, I thrust a bottle of vodka from a distillery in Idaho into his hands, presenting it as an offering.

"I'm so sorry we're late," I said.

Vince looked at the gift with something like disappointment.

Only the next day did I realize that Vince had given up drinking years ago.

There was something frosty in our time with Vince, and I was trying to find a way to puncture the rudeness of being a late-arriving houseguest. That afternoon, as I sat at the kitchen table as Vince returned from golf, he joined me and asked me what I had been learning.

"You know, it's less about politics than I thought it would be. It's really more of a search for meaning," I said as I regaled anecdotes from Skeets and from Earthhaven.

Sitting in the kitchen, Vince started talking about losing his daughter unexpectedly nearly ten years ago. "Talk about searching for meaning—I tried everything. Christianity, Buddhism."

Suddenly Vince was talking about his own search for meaning in the wake of unbearable tragedy. Michael and I listened enraptured as he got deep with us, talking about grief, loss, and healing.

I sensed that there was something unexpectedly cathartic in being able to have such an intimate conversation with two strangers. As Vince concluded his learnings, "ultimately you can only live in the present," I felt some relief that maybe we had been vindicated for our late arrival and inappropriate gift with an offering of a different kind: listening.

The night before we left for Los Angeles, Michael knocked on the door of the bedroom I was staying in at Vince's house. Michael entered the room with a small, wrapped gift in his hand.

"I got you something in Japan."

I looked at him, touched.

"It's nothing huge, it's just something cultural," he said, shrugging and handing me the gift.

I opened it up and found a small clay egg-shaped figurine.

"It's a *Daruma*," he explained. "You paint one eye with a goal in mind, and then every time you see it, you meditate on it until you finish that goal, and then you paint the other eye. I thought it would be good for your book."

I was really moved. I gave Michael a hug and packed the *Daruma* away in my suitcase, safely nestled in my socks.

As we drove towards Los Angeles, the two of us continued with the topic of loss. I finally started to tell Michael what I had been bottling up since Wyoming. As Michael asked questions, I instantly started to feel catharsis. We started to talk about people we had lost, drifted from, broken with. We talked about our time in college, when we both dated two best friends. I had been quietly wrestling with guilt for years of how I had handled the breakup after it turned long-distance, and I realized that Michael was someone who understood, having been through the same thing. These failures contributed to my sense that I needed an off-ramp.

"These relationships, they were just so raw. No holds barred."

"Totally," Michael said. "I mean, I told her things about my family I'd never told anyone. And the thing is… I don't think I'll ever share that with another partner again."

"That intensity."

"Exactly. And I feel bad," Michael continued, "I feel bad for how things ended."

"Same. But the environments we were in weren't germane for our growth," I added.

"Right. But it doesn't mean that they weren't important to us. We wouldn't be the people we are today without them."

The shared experience of our college relationships coming to an end helped me have a realization: the reason these people meant so much to us was because we needed each other so badly at that point. They were maybe the first people we were truly vulnerable with, the people who got to see us as adult larvae, helpless in so many ways, but loved us anyway. We didn't have the vocabulary or self-understanding to know what we wanted, how to articulate it, or how to be gentle with someone else in getting it. As I admitted my failures, Michael did the same. It was a healing conversation.

I thought of all of the realizations I'd had in Tennessee. In Wyoming. Maybe you had to drive across the country to have thoughts like this. To have growth.

Michael drove; I continued wading in my regret. Looking to turn it into a positive, I drafted a text to my ex.

"I'm in Arizona wrapping up this trip with Michael and just wanted to say we both miss you, and I really hope you're doing well."

I didn't want anything in return; I just wanted to offer a gentle touch from afar to acknowledge the role he played in my life. I didn't even care about the response.

Michael and I stopped at a gas station and switched driving duties. He snoozed as I drove through the dark mountains. Perhaps it was as Vince said: we can only live in the present, and in the present I had a lot to be grateful for. I looked over at Michael. I'd hoped I'd find love on the trip, but in many ways I hadn't been ready to accept the most profound love of all: the love of a friend who sees you as you are.

THE WEST COAST

I MOVED to California right out of college. I really don't know why. Upon graduating from Northwestern, I felt compelled to try my luck out west in Los Angeles. I had a lead on a job to be the assistant to the head of Universal Studios, a position being vacated by a friend from college, and I thought the entertainment industry was where I would make my mark.

"She wants a girl," my friend warned.

"Wait 'til she meets me," I said, thinking of how Warbucks changed his mind about wanting a male orphan after meeting Annie.

I moved to Los Angeles, interviewed for the position, and didn't get it. Realizing that perhaps I should've been less overconfident, I started looking for temporary work to pay rent. As someone who had only ever had part-time hourly work, my search led me to Craigslist. I saw a post for "actor, good with families" for $50 an hour. Deciding it couldn't possibly be for pornography and drooling at the hourly rate, I responded to the ad and was given the address for "training." I arrived at a mansion in the Los Feliz neighborhood, only to be met by a frantic woman who intercepted me before I rang the doorbell and took me to a shed in the backyard. Inside the shed was a small cot, a bunsen burner, and enough clown costumes to supply a circus. I realized this woman lived here. She sat me down next to two other girls around my age and promptly began teaching us the proper ways to tie balloon animals.

Thus began my four-day stint as a birthday party clown. Whether it was providing entertainment for a Mexican church gathering where no one spoke English or an aristocratic French toddler's birthday party, I experienced highs (being fed tamales by the pastor and his wife while looking like Tim Curry in "It") and lows (being punched in the face by a crying French toddler). I eventually found work as an associate producer at the production company Magical Elves (which produced my favorite competition show, *Top Chef*). There, I met Tracey and was grateful for every day I didn't have to dress up as a clown.

As I returned to Los Angeles to deliver Michael safely to his old apartment, I remembered how much I loathed the transactional nature of an industry town run on attention. After dropping off Michael's luggage, we were invited to a watch party for Trump's State of the Union address at a local bar in West Hollywood. The event was organized by a group of friends from the Hillary Clinton campaign. One of these friends was Brett, who would be my next travel companion up the west coast. Brett was a former college baseball player turned Democratic digital guru, though he looked much more like the former; Brett had dark hair, a serious face, and the forearms of an athlete. His dark features made multiple people on the campaign mistake him for a Cuban, giving him ample opportunity to display his non-existent Spanish language skills.

As we sat out on a garden patio and welcomed members of the Los Angeles Democratic Party, we watched Trump's State of the Union address projected onto a screen against the vine-covered wall. The jeers at his statements from the crowd took me back to the rally I had attended months ago, where similar jeers had been evoked from the crowd at the mention of the "Do Nothing Democrats." I played along, but it made me feel sad how issues of life and death were a game of political football.

After the speech—we were all anxious to hear from Stacey Abrams who was giving the rebuttal—a young man on a skateboard rolled up to the event. He donned a backwards cap covered in metal spikes over long, oily hair, and I saw a slight sheen of makeup on his face. He sat down in an empty chair next to me and Brett and started to converse with us. Lee, as he was called, started asking about our involvement in the party. I told him about my work on the Hillary campaign and my travels, and he started talking about how he got involved with the Democratic Party through sex work advocacy. I didn't know if "being involved in sex work advocacy" meant being a sex worker himself, but I was interested in what he had to say. We conversed about his advocacy during the rebuttal, and at the end of the night, he gave me a card and asked me to look him up if I was interested in talking more.

I sent a text the next day, asking if he wanted to have an interview to continue our conversation.

"Sure. My place or a coffee shop?"

I didn't know how to respond, not wanting to assume that he himself was a sex worker, but I also knew that for recording purposes a quiet place was the best place. Still, I took the cautious route and suggested the coffeeshop.

For the sake of clarity, this was probably for the best. Lee was indeed a sex worker, and that was part of what he wanted to discuss with me.

"So you said you're writing a book about people around the country?"

"That's right."

"Well I feel like this is an important perspective, an unheard perspective. Personally, I've always had an interest in working with sex workers. I am a sex worker," Lee said, sitting in the brightly-lit, crowded West Hollywood coffee shop.

"I don't think I've ever met a sex worker before," I admitted.

He laughed. "You don't *think* you have. But I'm sure you have. It comes in different shapes and forms, but not everyone does it full time. I do it full time."

He explained how he fell into sex work while working at a non-profit organization in Hollywood while paying off student loans.

"It started as something I did just to, you know, pay bills," he said, clutching his skateboard in his hand. "But then I realized I was good at it. I mean, good with people, you know. Emotionally."

Lee explained how a bipartisan bill to help those who were sex trafficked, spearheaded by Democratic lawmakers like Kamala Harris, had actually harmed sex workers like him. "Basically it sounds good on the surface, just massive funding of human trafficking services, but the piece that really affected sex workers is it essentially shut down the advertising platforms that sex workers use specifically, like BackPage and Craigslist. But the law holds websites accountable if they facilitate human trafficking services. So that effectively made all these websites liable, and they said we're not going to have any liability, so they shut them down. But it also extended beyond that to websites that sex workers used to vet clients. There's a list of blacklisted clients, for example, message boards where sex workers exchange information that's relevant to their safety. Yeah. So those websites also were compelled to remove themselves to avoid legal liability under this law. So it's pushed people back to street-based sex work life, which is so much less safe than, you know, indoor sex work, whatever."

He leaned back and sipped the coffee.

"It just sucks when you have to suck a dick to pay rent and you don't have any way to vet who you're interacting with."

Brett hopped in my car later that afternoon. Over tacos, I told him the story of Lee.

Brett shook his head. "Dude, you need to be more careful."

"What?"

"You almost went to that guy's house! What did you think he thought was going on?"

177

"I really think he just wanted someone to listen to him," I said, wondering if what Brett said was true. "I did buy coffee though."

Brett shrugged. "Fair enough."

Brett and I started our drive up north. Our plan was to dip into Reno (population 246,500) by way of Lake Tahoe to check Nevada off the list. Driving through the mountains, a terrible storm was brewing. Instead of stopping, I was adamant about not losing my chance to pass into the state of Nevada. We spent one night in Reno, crashing on the couch of a friend from college who worked for Tesla. Reno felt like a faded '80s version of Vegas, and I was ready to see something new as we drove through the mountains again and back into the state of California.

Brett and I were going to stay in Oceano (population 7,601), near Pismo beach where a friend of mine was working at The Great American Melodrama & Vaudeville Theater. Sara was a music director for the production of *A Christmas Carol* I had been in with Julia, and she was absolutely buzzing to have me come visit this theatre.

"It's one of the oldest melodrama theaters in the country," Sara explained as she gave me a tour of the theatre, which looked more like an old saloon connected to the American Legion performance hall I had danced at in Nashville. I looked up at the posters on the wall, advertising shows for the season. Some I had heard of, like "Steel Magnolias" which we would be seeing later that evening, but also new musicals like "Pappa Pia!" (the paternal version of *Mamma Mia!*, I assumed). When the play started, we found it to be a rowdy atmosphere, where the cast had a pre-show singalong before the dramatic play. During intermission, we found the actors manning the bar, pouring pitchers of beer for the audience. The character that would soon be deceased in the play handed me a pitcher of Blue Moon and winked.

"It's on the house."

Great American, indeed. I loved every second of it and felt a weird pride in the cultural tradition of Vaudeville that America had birthed. Something about the dichotomy of the seriousness of the play and the silliness of watching Brett sing along to "You Are My Sunshine" helped me see that Brett probably needed some mental space from the work of politics.

As we drove up the Pacific Coast Highway, Brett was agonizing over the question on everyone in politics' mind in 2019: which Democratic candidate was going to successfully nab the nomination and/or who would be the best to work for?

Brett and I drove, trying to diagnose the cultural moment. On the spectrum from Bernie Sanders to Joe Biden, tens of candidates had already declared or were heavily staffing up.

"I just want someone who will keep their eye on the ball," I said. "Talk about the things that actually matter to people, pocketbook issues, not divide us further."

Brett shook his head. "Unfortunately, it's all about firing people up. Going viral. That's how you raise money, that's how you break through."

Brett and I decided to stay away from San Francisco, despite the fact that his sister lived there; I had only been to the city once, and it had been a Truth or Consequences-like experience. During the summer before I departed from living in California, my frequent travel companion (also named Ryan) and I decided we might soak up more San Fran flavor and save money in the notoriously expensive city by booking through CouchSurfing.com, which allows travelers to stay on strangers' couches for free. The only person with an availability for our dates was a nudist named "Zeus."

Looking at his profile, I was extremely skeptical. "No," I said.

Ryan, pouring another glass of wine, protested. "But Zeus has over 400 positive reviews!"

"So?"

"Most people only have three or four; he has the most of anyone."

It was true. Guests were calling him a "life-changing" person who showed them the "real San Francisco."

"Let's wait it out. I'm sure we can find something better."

We were not able to find something better, so two nights before the trip, we pulled the trigger on this "once in a lifetime opportunity."

We arrived at the San Francisco airport with deliberate directions from Zeus about how to get to his apartment. We picked up a housewarming bottle of rum (he said he enjoyed making cocktails) and walked to his apartment, noticing that the cleanliness of the lovely downtown had started to fade.

"Hm, there are bars on the windows!"

"Does it smell like urine?"

"Is that man shooting up heroin?"

We walked into the middle of the Tenderloin neighborhood and passed a delegation of Vietnamese missionaries helping a man lying on the sidewalk with no pants.

We arrived at the apartment door and texted Zeus.

He responded quickly. "Check in at the front desk. 2502."

We took our suitcases into the elevators and got another text. "Shoes off, clothes off at the door."

"… what?"

He replied with a link to his FAQ. Upon further inspection, we saw a crucial line that we had overlooked: "Guests are not allowed to wear clothes."

Ryan and I stared at each other, horrified. "Should we leave?"

Ryan, a plan-follower, looked panicked. "Where else would we go?"

Peer pressure is a funny thing, and next thing Ryan and I knew we were both sitting naked, cross-legged on a tiny leather couch in front of an awkward, naked man in the middle of a tiny studio apartment.

"So…" Zeus said, standing naked in front of us, as though he was waiting for us to start a business meeting.

"Oh! We brought you some rum, because you, uh, said in your bio that you enjoy making cocktails."

"Oh, rum... goes with... coke, right?"

We blinked at him. "Yes."

"I think I might have some... I shouldn't be drinking cuz I'm on muscle relaxers, but..."

Zeus opened the rum and rummaged around a bare fridge for a few scraggly ice cubes.

We learned that Zeus worked at a corporate job, had been a nudist for five months, and was a self-described rapper. On his wall, he had multiple notecards where he had posted his short-term goals ("sell 100 rap albums") and long-term goals ("buy mom house" and "open gay hedonist resort") on the wall. When asked what the sleeping arrangement was, he casually said, "my guests always sleep in bed with me."

We noticed a whiteboard next to his bed with notes from his other guests: "thanks for having me" and "thanks for showing me around San Fransisco" and "thanks for being my first gay sex partner." Ryan and I looked at each other in horror. After further chitchat, Zeus mercifully instructed us to put on our clothes and head up to the roof, where a beautiful panoramic view of San Francisco was laid out before us.

"So I just want to lay down some ground rules. You're not allowed in the apartment unless I'm there."

"Seems fair."

"Saturday night I will be attending a sex and drugs party and won't come home, which means you have to come along."

"Oh," we both said, nodding. "Yeah, that's fine."

"We need to get out," I whispered to Ryan as we got back in the elevator.

But instead of bringing us back to the apartment where all of our possessions sat captive, Zeus declared it was time for dinner and he was in the mood for Thai. We told Zeus we needed to go to a birthday party and asked him if he knew any good restaurants in the Castro, hoping he would take the hint that he was not invited.

"I do. I'll take you there."

The goal was to shake him, but now he was leading us to the metro stop through the seemingly-dodgy area that was his neighborhood.

We arrived at a Thai restaurant. After a very awkward dinner, where he talked about his journey to becoming a nudist (but apparently only in his apartment) five months ago, we again told him we were going to our friend Em's birthday party. He said he'd be joining us.

We arrived at the bar for the party and greeted Em, who (understandably) asked, "who the hell is this guy?"

"We decided to CouchSurf," I said, hearing the ridiculousness of what I was saying for the first time.

"Why didn't you stay with me?" Em said, incredulous. "My spare room and couch are being used now, but I could've figured something out."

"I don't know, it was all so last minute!"

"Where are you staying?"

"The Tenderloin?"

Em looked horrified.

"Is that bad?"

"It's one of the most dangerous neighborhoods in America. Which cross streets?"

I pulled up my phone and showed her. Em looked up at me. "You need to get out. Now." Zeus (fully clothed) was sipping a beer in the corner by himself, muscle relaxers be damned.

I immediately stepped outside and called my friend's parents whom I normally wouldn't have asked for such a big, last-minute favor. "We're having a housing crisis... can we stay with you?" They agreed, so long as we were there by 10. It was 8:30. Our bags were still at Zeus's.

We had to plot our escape.

We told Zeus that we were tired and wanted to go home... but he shook his head. "I'm meeting some friends. You have to come with me."

We were forced to go with Zeus to a surly gay bar to meet a wild-looking woman who looked like a former Broadway dame and a man who looked like a lumberjack. Though we were anxious, Zeus said he wouldn't leave until he finished his drink, which he was drinking very, very slowly, making sly comments about the sleeping arrangements for the evening. As I went out to make calls to our new hosts, Zeus started asking Ryan explicit, probing questions.

I got a text from Ryan. "HELP!!!"

Finally, around 9:55, I grabbed Zeus's drink and downed it. "There's an Uber waiting downstairs. Let's go."

When we arrived back in The Tenderloin (scarier after dark) and got to the apartment, Zeus went into the doorless bathroom to disrobe. We stayed clothed, clutching our suitcases.

"You tell him!" he whispered to me.

"You booked it, you have to tell him," I hissed at Ryan.

Zeus came out and saw us still clothed. "What's going on?"

"So! Our friend Em had a surprise extra room, so we'll get out of your hair," Ryan said brightly.

Zeus stared stonily at him.

"Yeah, we thought this might be easier, so you don't have to worry about us with your, uh, sex and drugs party," Ryan said, flashing a winning smile. "But thanks so much for everything!"

The naked man glared at us, incredulous at what he was hearing.

"I have never been so disrespected in my life!" hissed Zeus. "How dare you leave unceremoniously."

Finding myself feeling guilty, I jumped in, hoping I could be the good cop to Ryan's bad cop. I threw my hands up to my temples. "Oh no! Oh no! I feel so bad!"

Ryan stared at me.

"If you're going to leave, just leave," Zeus said, sounding like we had canceled Christmas.

"Okay... bye!"

We opened the door, pulled our bags out of the apartment, and ran to the elevator.

"What were you doing in there??" Ryan yelled as I called an Uber. "Why did you say you wanted to stay?"

"I was *acting!*"

Ryan rolled his eyes.

At nearly 11pm, the streets of the Tenderloin were crowded with people, who instantly surrounded us, exactly as my phone died.

"Shit!" I yelled, just as someone asked if we were looking for a "vacancy."

Miraculously, a yellow cab zoomed past us, and we waved our hands wildly as it swerved onto the curb, scooped us up, and delivered us to safety to Knob Hill.

As we sat in the cab, panting with disbelief at our escape, Ryan's phone dinged.

"I just got a review from CouchSurfing."

Ryan opened the email. Zeus had fired off an angry review of us, calling both of us "nice boys" but "total couch-surfing amateurs" who "left unceremoniously."

Ryan laughed.

"What?"

"He still gave us 3 out of 5 stars."

"Next time we couch surf, we'll use my account," I said, leaning my head on the window. "I don't want the next nudist to think we'll leave unceremoniously."

The next stop was Bend, Oregon (population 93,917). I was meeting with Sally Russell, the mayor of the town. We met in a small coffee shop.

"Someone asked me to run for City Council and I was like no way," Sally said. "But then a friend said, 'think globally and act locally.' And that's what did it for me. I don't think of myself as a politician. I think of myself as a consensus-builder, a community-builder."

Sally sighed and sipped her coffee.

"One of the biggest environmental wins in the Northwest was signed by Republicans. I think that's a really important message for people who think certain wins can only come from one group or another. A lot of the best ideas for our communities come from where we meet in the middle. It's harder and harder to live in that world."

When Sally was elected mayor, she left an open seat on the City Council. Sally told us how she had been pilloried by progressives in the town for nominating a pro-business man to the City Council rather than a more diverse pick.

"We had 39 applications. Of them, 25 were men and 11 were women. One Hispanic man. One woman of color. So we went through the whole interview process. We got down to four or five finalists. I spent a lot of time vetting people. I did a lot of character references, beyond the references provided. I wanted to think of who had the skills to knit that council together. And I picked a white man, instead of the woman of color who was in the final three. And you know, a lot of people accused me of unconscious bias. They look at me as someone who took the easy road. But I think of myself as someone who took the hard road. I stood with the Hispanic community after Trump was elected. I was a woman who supported the Welcoming City Resolution in 2017. But I also have a master's in business. I've run businesses. I've put together teams. This was a business decision for the community. But people put a lot of value judgments on it. But I wasn't lobbied by anyone with an R next to their name. I did the best I could with what I had.

"Do you think the outrage will fizzle out?"

"Time will tell. Our community is changing, our country is changing. I can just try to understand my community."

Driving across the state through the mountains towards Portland (population 641,162), Brett and I encountered another snowstorm. This time, however, we were stopped by a patrol car and required to put snow chains on Belinda. In near white-out conditions, Brett and I took turns trying to link the snow chains around all four wheels, returning to the car to warm up while the other braved the winter. As we finally got the snow chains on, Belinda vibrated with the friction of the metal links wrapped along her wheels. As we descended the mountains, the blizzard turned to sleet, then to rain. The car was still shaking with the grinding of the metal chains against the asphalt, and I noticed a small crack begin to form on the corner of the windshield.

Brett looked at it too. "What is that?"

"Just a smudge, I think."

But we watched as the small crack began to grow, spreading from the bottom corner of the windshield and snaking its way across the glass.

"Not a smudge, Ryan."

By the time I realized the vibrations from the snow chains were causing the crack to grow, it was too late. Belinda's windshield now looked dangerously likely to shatter.

"Welcome to the journey, Mr. Crack," Brett said.

Though the windshield did not shatter, Mr. Crack would remain a source of anxiety for the rest of the trip.

In Portland, we stayed with a local fisherman who introduced us to Rex Burkholder, an author of *The Activist's Toolkit*, a guide for getting things done on a local level. We met in the living room of his home as he discussed the impetus for writing the book.

"So I wrote this book and updated it after 2016, when... certain things happened. Because, especially now, how do you deal with that sense of ineffectiveness and futility in the face of major forces? There are great philosophers of the past who gave us guidance for, you know, how do you deal with the fact that we're all going to die? How do you deal with the fact that time is so short? You live life. How do you fill it up? How do you make yourself useful?"

"What do you think people nowadays don't understand about activism?"

Rex scratched his chin. "Well, it's kind of like the word politician. Where it's been disparaged and given a very negative connotation that somehow being an activist means you are a different creature and probably not very nice."

I dropped Brett off at the Portland airport and made my way up to Seattle (population 733,919). I parked my car at my Aunt Nancy and Uncle Gary's home (with my mom's six sisters, I really did have housing in at least six states covered). I was leaving the next day for the states off the mainland, and my Aunt Nancy and Uncle Gary took me to a party at a neighbor's home, where we talked about the incredible growth of Seattle and the implementation of light rail transportation solutions across the city. I was close with my aunt and uncle; when I was a junior in high school, I had gone to the Canadian boarding school that their daughters had attended across the bay from Seattle on Vancouver Island. I had often stayed with them on holidays and their house on Puget Sound felt like another home. My decision to go to boarding school was a bizarre one and due to a combination of fortuitous events post-coming out. At 16, I was constantly walking on eggshells to not discuss the topic banished into storage until my eighteenth birthday. I began pursuing the idea of going somewhere else for school. I was desperate to find a place I felt I belonged, and I busied myself researching scholarships for performing arts schools across the country. However, one day my mom, sensing my restlessness, approached me with a compromise.

My two cousins from Seattle had been studying at the Canadian boarding school Brentwood College for the past four years, and it was considered a reputable school internationally. Brentwood had eventually funneled both of them into the medical school at St.

Andrews in Scotland, the alma mater of Prince William. My parents allowed me to put in an application to the school in February, and by April I was accepted. With a promise of financial help from an earmark in Grandma's will, I decided that I had to advance my plot away from my Catholic education and the half-truths I was operating in. Not really considering the full repercussions of escaping Rockford, I decided to accept my spot, and I was off to school 2,154 miles away from my problems.

Suddenly, I was a Midwest kid from a basic Catholic high school, thrust amidst the higher echelon of Canadian society. I instantly missed my family and friends in Rockford terribly. People I had relied on were no longer accessible; Wi-Fi shut off promptly at nine, and in the moments when I felt most alone there wasn't anyone I could call. It was a period of loneliness, though I eventually got my bearings. But the idea that I was living two lives, not really rooted anywhere, lasted with me even a decade later.

As I returned to the Seattle airport, the familiar sights reminded me of the scared 16-year-old I was, returning from Christmas Vacation or Spring Break. I thought of how I would reinvent myself in the airport, shed who I was at home to become who I had to be to survive in the new environment. As I waited and boarded the plane for Alaska, I felt I was similarly heading into an unknown territory. I had never been to America's largest state, and I had no idea what to expect. I boarded the plane to Anchorage, and I dreamed of Brentwood and my formative year in Canada as I snoozed on the plane.

I was staying with a family from the Midwest that a friend had put me in touch with. Carole, Bud, and their son Luke welcomed me into their home in Anchorage (population 288,121). Luke was legally blind and well taken care of by his nurturing parents who still had their Midwestern hospitality.

"You'd be amazed at the number of Midwest transplants who

end up in Alaska," they told me as they fit me into rubber boots to help me brave the snow.

They were lovely hosts, taking me to all the local restaurants and even buying me tickets for a local community theatre production. The first day, they took me out into the car and drove me north out of Anchorage. The mountains towered over us on the left and the frozen water spread out on our right. It was desolate and beautiful. Carole, Bud, Luke and I made it to the Alyeska Ski Resort in Girdwood (population 1,037), where we ordered Alaska-brewed beers and sat by a roaring fire. As I looked up at the ski lifts climbing up into the mountains, a part of me wished I had come in the summer. I could only imagine the blues, grays, and whites of the winter landscape lush with green.

The next afternoon, I met John, the head of the Alaska Democratic party, at his office in the outskirts of Anchorage. John was a bald man with an infectious intensity when he talked.

"You're the head of a Democratic Party in a red state; what does that teach you about what people want from Democrats?"

"Well, I've never worked in a blue state. This is actually the most blue state I've worked in because we control the State House here. We don't control the state Senate, but we did have the governor's mansion in a weird arrangement of the Democrats supporting an Independent. The lieutenant governor was a Democrat."

"So it's not as ideological here in Alaska?"

"Absolutely not. People come to a party for different reasons. Some care deeply about an issue or some people might care about a particular candidate, right? You know, Bill Walker was governor of Alaska. He's no great progressive. I mean, no one would ever accuse him of being liberal. He's personally pro-life. But he was absolutely committed to making sure that women continued to have good health care choices in Alaska, and he was certainly better than the alternative. Reality sets in pretty quickly. This is a man who expanded Medicare and Medicaid and gave 40,000 Alaskans health care. A man who was a Republican who became an independent but said, 'I don't buy that conservative mantra. This is good for Alaska.' And so that was a positive. A Republican governor wouldn't do that here."

"So he was basically more willing to compromise."

"Exactly," John said, nodding vigorously. "People cringe when people use the word compromise. But it works. Look at Massachusetts. They have a Republican governor. Everyone loves Charlie Baker. The difference is, I would argue, Charlie Baker is probably not a right-wing religious zealot, you know, that's what we end up with here in Alaska."

After speaking to John, I got connected to a local community theatre called TBA, helmed by Isaac and Wendy, two artists dedicated to bringing theatre to Alaska. I went to a rehearsal for a production of *West Side Story* at a local union hall and watched as a mixture of people performed a spirited rendition of "America."

After the rehearsal, Isaac and Wendy took me on a tour of different theatre facilities in the area. I asked them about the role that their theatre played in the community.

"It's really about nurturing artists, but it's also about fostering an environment where people create something together," said Isaac.

Wendy nodded. "We have a white Mormon playing Tony and a gay Filipino as Bernardo. And now they're best friends. In what other universe does that happen?"

Isaac and Wendy told me that they had a friend in Hawaii, Jess, who would show me around when I visited, again demonstrating how theatre people tended to be some of the most generous and kind I met on the trip. I didn't realize the tight bond between residents of Alaska and Hawaii, as they felt somewhat set apart from others in the lower 48 states, and apparently flying between Alaska and Hawaii was more common than I thought.

I was only able to spend three days in Hawaii. I had been put in touch with a family who lived in a condo on the shores of Honolulu (population 345,510); when I contacted them for the first time, I heard intense trepidation in their voices about letting me stay in their home. "You can stay for one night," they said. When I finally met Kathy, a white lawyer and Ron, her Native Hawaiian husband, the chemistry was so good they let me stay for all three.

"We thought you might've been a crazy person."

"I am," I said, as I took a pillow and a blanket out to the daybed on their balcony and slept outside. I woke up to rainbows over the bay every morning, and I never slept inside for the rest of my time in Hawaii.

Ron woke me up early on my second day to take me canoe surfing. I had no idea what canoe surfing meant or if I would be any good at it, but when we met up with his friends—all Native Hawaiian guys in their forties—they demonstrated how to quickly row out to catch a wave and allow the momentum of the ocean to propel the boat back to shore. It was a tremendous effort followed by a placid rush. I absolutely loved it.

I decided Hawaii was one of the perfect places to face my fears; for Christmas, I had been gifted an "experience" in one of the 50 states and I decided that I wanted to try skydiving for the first time here in Hawaii. As I faced my mortality sitting in the small plane, I marveled at the lushness of the mountains below, the shades of turquoise of the ocean. Hawaii, I decided, was far too beautiful for me to deserve to live there. As I heard my name called and crouched on the edge of the open airplane door, I thought about the very real prospect of my demise, but then thought of seeming like a coward and backing out. I tipped forward and fell into the open air.

It is rare to feel three completely new sensations in such a short span of time—I found myself tumbling through the air, not knowing which way was up, then feeling the wind resisting my free fall as my body stretched horizontally. Right as my body made sense of both of these sensations, I felt the sudden tug and resistance of a parachute opening, then the jarring leisure of gliding down over a whale-filled bay. As I hit the ground, the man strapped to my back unattached himself from me and asked me if I knew I was screaming the entire time.

"Oh no… what was I saying?"

"You kept saying 'this life! This life!' as though you couldn't believe it was real," he said chuckling. He told me that I had the look in my eye of a changed man, a rube who became a true skydiving believer in midair.

I returned to the monotony of the Marriott Waikiki lobby, trying to wrap my head around what had just happened. As I enjoyed the free outlets and listened to a family of tourists chase their youngest toddler around the lobby, I got a text from Jess—the connection made by my friends in Anchorage—that she was outside ready to pick me up.

I found her sitting in a gray Mini Cooper. She was a blonde lady with a spirit of infectious chill, and I instantly felt at home with her. She was an employee in the University of Hawaii theatre department, and she was taking me across the island to the family party of Hailiopua—a fellow faculty member and theatre-maker at the university. Her entire family was made up of Kanaka Maoli-Hawaiian speakers and they were all gathering to celebrate her son's 21st birthday.

We arrived at a state park and learned that the party was being thrown on ancestral lands that they had recently won from the government in court. When I arrived, Hailiopua, a dark-haired woman in a sleeveless summer dress, started introducing me to her family. I had the familiar feeling of being a clear outsider, but I didn't have time to waste feeling awkward. I had learned the only way to break this momentary lull was to start asking questions. I learned that Haili's family was born on this part of the island and she and her husband both worked at the university. Her husband took me to the shore and started pointing out different sections of the island, telling me about water disputes with farmers growing taro leaves. He pointed out to sacred islands in the bay but said with a twinkle in his eye that Hawaiians don't need much of an excuse to make something sacred.

"I just need to say a few words, and this party could be sacred!"

Hailiopua's son, cousins, and friends were starting to go out on paddle boards and kayaks. One of them tentatively asked if I wanted to join. I agreed and helped push the boats into the bay.

Ten minutes later, I was out in the middle of the bay with six college seniors. Each of them was at the university, either studying Hawaiian Language or Culture. They went fluently between speaking Hawaiian and English but were clearly not doing it for my sake.

Remembering how Alaskans had felt about the lower 48, I asked them what they thought of people on the mainland.

An instantaneous murmur went around the group. "You mean the colonists?"

They gave me a quick recap of Hawaii's history. In short, Americans orchestrated a *coup d'etat* to overthrow the Queen of Hawaii, and there was no formal treaty that made Hawaii a territory, making the annexation…

"Illegal."

My own naiveté was on full display. When I thought of Hawaii, I thought of… pineapple. Surfing. Hula. *The Descendants*.

"Do you see any benefits to being a part of America? The military protection or—?"

"The *military*?" They all seemed appalled. They talked about seeing tanks everywhere on the island, to the point where it doesn't even phase them anymore. "Plus what they did, bombing sacred islands. Destroying the aquifers. They don't care. They pretend to care, even at the university. But they still build their buildings and bases and observatories wherever they want."

"I'm a huge supporter of the Independence Movement," a boy said, sipping a Miller Light.

The Hawaiian Independence movement? Had I missed something in history class?

"They don't teach this stuff here either," a girl sighed sadly.

Just then, a sea turtle broke the surface. They all started murmuring excitedly in Hawaiian, but I picked up on a common word: "*ea.*"

Haili's son turned to me. "*Ea* is a word that means independence and solidarity, but it also means breath."

A shirtless guy on a kayak said, "it's a metaphor. The water in the bay, that's being in America. All of the capitalism, all of that stuff we have to exist in. But turtles need to come up for air. Get *ea*. That's what we do when we come together. We speak our language, we have our traditions."

A girl on the paddle-board agreed. "Turtles lay eggs on land. That's like us. We're born out of American society. But we have to live *in* it."

I didn't have my phone out there, and Jess was waiting, so we finished our Miller Lights and rowed back to shore. I hated myself that there had been too many unfamiliar names for me to remember, but hopefully they knew that I went out on the water a naive mainlander and came back slightly wiser to America's role in colonizing language, culture, and resources.

Jess drove me back into town. I had plans to meet up with my brother's friend from high school, Benny, who was an army captain stationed in Hawaii. We met at a Hooters in downtown Honolulu, and Benny gushed about the mansion he and "the boys" from the military lived in together, the parties on the beach, the awesome drills they ran. When I asked about the Hawaiian Independence movement I had learned about, he said he wasn't familiar.

I wondered if I could've found a bigger contrast between Haili's son's party and Hooters. I ordered wings as the bartender came over and sat on Benny's lap and kissed him on the cheek, giggling as he played with her hair.

"This is my girlfriend!" Benny said, sounding thrilled with his military life in Hawaii.

I sipped my beer and nodded as Benny and the bartender started making out. From canoe surfing to skydiving, from to *ea* to Hooters, Hawaii certainly contained multitudes.

THE MOUNTAINS, THE PLAINS & THE PRAIRIES

I ARRIVED BACK in Seattle and picked up my car. I headed for Montana, a gigantic state to traverse, and a state where I thought I knew virtually no one.

Nine states left. Scheduled interviews were fewer and farther between. This was fine by me. I was exhausted, tired of packing and unpacking constantly, and ready to be done. I naively antici-pated this journey would bring big clarifying answers and solve my malaise, but now I just felt tired. It didn't help that it was mid-February and my little Belinda had proved to be a novice winter vehicle. Driving through Washington, I felt—for the first time since the beginning of the journey—that I was truly alone.

The eastern part of Washington was flat. The lushness of the coast was replaced by craggy brown foothills. I had decided to drive to Missoula (population 74,822), with no particular agenda there besides Brett's assertion that it was a town I could fall in love with. But I wasn't feeling like falling in love; I arrived in Missoula after dark. I drove around campus, feeling cold and sorry for myself. I sat in a gas station, looking at potential Airbnbs. I smiled as I saw one in a refurbished school bus. A buzz from the cupholder—I looked down at my phone. It was my dad.

"Where are you staying tonight?" My story from Truth and Consequences had rattled him.

"Currently," I checked the listing again, "looks like I'm going to be staying in a refurbished school bus!" I said, trying to sound chipper. "Cool experience, huh?"

"I'm booking you a hotel."

"No, it's a cool experience!"

"Does it have heat?"

"Let me check."

It did not.

I arrived at the hotel. It was called the "C'mon Inn" and built to resemble a giant log cabin on the outside. I walked into the foyer, which was vaulted like a cathedral made out of painted wooden logs. The lobby was also filled with no fewer than a dozen hot tubs.

"Are these available for use?" I asked the receptionist.

The woman at the desk coughed then nodded. "Until ten."

I returned to the lobby in my swimsuit and towel. I was the only person in the lobby, which resembled a hot tub emporium more than a hotel. Unsure of what to do, I tentatively put my hands in the hot tub. A staff member passed by.

"Can I just… get in?" I asked.

He looked at me like it was obvious one should sit in a hot tub in a hotel lobby. "Yep."

I sat in the hot water as guests checked in. I looked to my left where the breakfast station sat waiting for the morning shift. Something about hot tubs and waffle makers didn't sit right with me; I resolved to pick food up on the road the next day.

I drove to Helena (population 33,120), the capital city. A blizzard was on its way, so I quickly got Thai food downtown and walked through the capitol building. Montana felt like a good contender for a place to live before I arrived, but the quick rush through wasn't endearing me to the state. Worse yet, I didn't have much of a game plan for the rest of Montana. I decided I would aim for Billings and start my lonely drive.

The mountains were looming large as I drove up and down steep inclines and into a blizzard. Not since my experience traversing Oregon with Brett was driving this treacherous, and my hands gripped the wheel tightly. Stopping at a rest stop to give myself a break, I started to look at places to stay. Right when it seemed I was going to have to book another hot tub hotel, I got a message on Facebook out of the blue from a girl I had gone to high school with but hadn't spoken to in nearly a decade.

"Saw Montana was on your list. My husband and I live outside of Great Falls, Montana. We'd love to host you."

I replied nearly immediately. "Are you free tonight?"

She read my message. Paused. "My husband isn't here, and the place is kind of a mess tonight... but you're welcome to stay with my friend who has a spare bedroom."

I was in. I drove towards Great Falls (population 58,835).

I met Dani and her friend at the Road House Diner downtown. I approached the table where she had a plate of french fries ready. She was a free-spirited high schooler at my buttoned-up Canadian boarding school, and I sensed a new adulthood about her as she told me about being a mom and the business she started with her husband, digging wells on construction sites.

"I'd love to talk to some of your workers," I said as the waitress approached.

"They're actually going out on site tomorrow if you want to go out and see for yourself," Dani said.

Tara, the friend who was hosting me, had been watching me pile hot sauce on my plate of fries. "Oh, if you like spicy, you gotta try the Widowmaker."

I looked at the menu. A burger topped with habanero, Serrano, and jalapeño peppers, ghost pepper bacon, and "Widow Sauce." Seemed like my kind of challenge.

"I warn you, it's *really* hot," said the waitress. "There's a reason they call it the Widowmaker. It makes people widows," she added unnecessarily.

I smiled. "I can take it."

"Love that confidence. I'll bring you some Hell Fries too, on the house."

As we waited for our food, we made plans for me to go out with some of the contractors in the field the next day. I had no idea what "well-drilling" entailed, but I hoped it was attached to somewhere warm.

It was not. The next morning, I woke up at Tara's to a text from Dani.

"Dress warm."

I looked out the window. It was starting to snow. I put on a heavy cardigan and a long dress coat and some leather boots. Warm enough, I thought. I burped suddenly, feeling the fire from the Widowmaker rise from the depths of my stomach.

When I showed up at their office, a large warehouse full of drilling equipment, the stubbled-faced men took one look at me and laughed. I could understand why. They were all bundled up in dirt-covered camo jackets, stained sweatpants, thick work boots. In my gray-speckled coat, turquoise cardigan, and preppy boots, I looked like the effete coastal elite I was trying not to be.

"This is Ryan," said Dani. "He goes to Oxford."

"In the U.K.," I said habitually, unhelpfully.

They smirked and looked me up and down. "Well, Ryan from Oxford is going to need to dress a little warmer."

They pulled out a box of miscellaneous warm clothes. I picked out a dirt-stained hoodie and discarded my coat in a back office, feeling like a fool. Tom, the lead engineer, came up with work boots for me. He took one look at my feet and turned around without a word. He returned with cowboy boots.

"These are women's," he said. "But I thought your feet were a little small for the other boots."

I didn't have time to feel offended; I was too busy feeling my stomach start to churn.

"Do you have a bathroom?" I asked.

Tom shook his head. "Out of service."

Tom introduced me to Antonio, the other engineer. They both looked alike: baseball caps, faces covered in stubble, shrewd eyes appraising me with intense amusement. Dani said goodbye as I got in the back of their pickup truck.

In the truck, Tom lit up a cigarette, and Antonio pulled out a canister of chewing tobacco. They spoke to each other for the first ten minutes about today's project. I gleaned they were drilling a well on a construction site. It was hard to concentrate. My stomach irritation had intensified to a full-on rebellion. I was going to ask if we could stop at a gas station, when Antonio addressed me.

"You dip?"

"Sorry?"

"Chew tobacco?"

"Uhhhh… no. I don't."

The snowflakes outside the truck were growing in their size and intensity.

"So why are you out here again? Dani didn't really explain."

"I'm going to all 50 states. Writing a book about—" I burped fire "—American democracy."

They looked at each other. "Why are you out here then?"

"I mean, you're a part of it. Trying to get as many perspectives as possible."

We drove in silence until we reached the site. By the time we got out of the car, it was a blizzard of biblical proportions. The site, to my dismay, was a flat piece of land on a hill in the middle of a neighborhood development. There were no buildings and certainly no bathrooms anywhere nearby.

The Montana wind stung as I opened the door to the car. It quickly became evident that, in my black hoodie and women's cowboy boots, I was not adequately dressed for the bitter winter weather. To make matters worse, I was on the verge of ruining my pants, and the only respite I had from worrying if my toes were freezing off was willing my entire digestive tract not to humiliate me in front of these men.

I looked at my phone. I had been outside for three minutes.

I stood uselessly to the side as Tom and Antonio started to use the drilling equipment. I had expected them to maybe explain what they were doing, but clearly it was evident.

"What are you building?" I yelled over the noise, trying to distract myself from my fears of frostbite and soiling myself.

"A well for a house," Antonio said. "Tom, I need the wrench."

"What do we do if we need the bathroom?"

Tom looked at me like I was insane. He walked over to the edge of the site, whipped it out and pissed in the snow. "That."

I braved standing outside for what felt like a hellish eternity as I was pumped by evil winds, stinging snow, and the wrath of the Widowmaker and Hell Fries. Finally, after a brave thirty-eight minutes, I asked for the keys to the truck from Tom. He seemed to have expected this. He handed me the keys in an off-handed way laced with judgment. I was in too much agony to care. I went and sat in the car, clutching my stomach and listening to the radio, eternally grateful for the warm air coming out of the vents.

About an hour later, Antonio and Tom returned to the car. They both turned around, smiling at me shivering in the back seat.

"Learn anything about democracy?"

"Not to order the Widowmaker before going out on a construction site."

Tom looked horrified. "You ordered the Widowmaker? From Road House?"

"Do you know how spicy that is?" said Tom.

"I do now."

They laughed. "Holy shit, man. Are you shitting your pants?"

I clenched my entire body. "It's getting close."

"Let's get you to lunch."

Luckily, despite the increasingly thick snow, Tom stepped on it on the way into town. We stopped at a small bar and grill called the Harvest Moon Saloon in downtown Belt, Montana (population 510). I darted to the bathroom, where I stayed for a long time.

I returned to the table, where a beer sat waiting for me.

"Perks of the job," Tom said, grinning. "Cheers."

I caved to pressure. I drank it.

The waitress came over and I ordered a burger.

"Can you bring some hot sauce?" I figured whatever they had would pale in comparison to the Widowmaker sauce.

Tom and Antonio looked disgusted and impressed. "You really like hot stuff, huh?"

"It's kind of a vice."

They looked at me with a newfound respect. I took another sip of beer, which opened up the conversation.

"All 50 states, huh?" said Antonio.

"Exactly."

"What number are we?"

"Uh... forty-two?"

"What kind of car are you driving?"

"A Toyota Prius."

They both groaned.

"What?"

"No man should drive that car."

I looked at them, for the first time a little affronted. Say what you want about me, but Belinda was off limits.

"What does that mean?"

"It's just..." they shrugged.

"Do you know how much gas it takes to drive to all 50 states?"

"Yeah, but..."

"I get 48 miles per gallon. Let's say I drive 25,000 miles on the trip." I started doing the math. "What's gas right now?"

Antonio thought about it. "A little over two dollars."

I punched some numbers in my phone calculator. "So I'll spend a little over a thousand on gas. For the whole trip. What does your car get?"

The food arrived. I could tell they saw my point.

As we ate, we talked about how they ended up working at AquaSource.

"I worked on oil rigs," said Tom. "Good money out there. Really good money."

"Why'd you leave?"

"They're getting soft. Now there are all these rules, rules about breaks, what you can and can't do on the job. When I was out there, it was hell, man. I didn't get breaks. But we drank and had a good time."

"You ever been out on a rig?"

"No, but I'd love to."

Antonio smiled at me. "Not many people want to go out on an oil rig."

"Just curious."

Antonio scratched his chin. "I feel like people look down on it. But then I tell them how much money I make, and they don't look down on it anymore."

"I don't look down on it."

Antonio nodded and bit off some of his sandwich. "I bought a lot with that money. I'm in the middle of building my second house with it."

"When will it be done?"

"Maybe in the spring. I'm kind of busy right now. Plus it's cold."

"Wait, are you *building* your house?"

They both found this funny.

"Yeah. I'm building it myself."

I was seriously impressed. I asked a bunch of questions about something as foreign to me as owning and building your own house. Antonio seemed proud.

"It's funny, man. I don't have a college degree. Barely finished high school," he said. "But I know how to do things. Things a lot of people don't know how to do. That's my education."

"And I have a degree… and in a lot of ways I'm a moron," I said.

They laughed.

On the way back to the office, the blizzard had become a full on "white out," according to Tom. Tom got a radio call from another truck that had gotten caught in a ditch.

"It's Johnny. We gotta go help pull him out."

I was extremely unhappy to hear this development, as I was looking forward to being back in Taylor's warm house in Great Falls. We turned the car around and headed out back into the storm.

We approached the extremely long driveway of a home that was having a well drilled. One of the pickup trucks sat in a ditch off to the side in an enormous snow bank. Tom pulled up to the struggling vehicle, opened his window, and called out.

"You okay, Johnny?"

Johnny opened his door. "You got a chain?"

"Yeah, I do. We've got three shovels. Let us help dig you out."

Both Tom and Antonio got out of the pickup. I wasn't sure if I was expected to man one of the three shovels, so I followed them into the blizzard.

The snow was a couple of feet deep. Tom handed me a shovel, and I plowed through the snow and into the ditch to help dig. Whatever cold I had experienced before, this was a new level. The snow was seeping into my women's cowboy boots. I noticed the other men had put on gloves, but I was too intent on proving that I was tough, that I was a man, to say anything about not having any of my own.

When the shoveling was adequately completed, Tom headed back to the car. I followed him, hoping for warmth. He saw me following, looked back and shook his head.

"We can't have any extra weight in the truck. Stay out here."

And so I watched as they chained up the truck to pull Johnny's pickup out of the snowy ditch. They tried driving forward, the truck barely lurching in the ditch. They tried again, momentarily tugging the nose of the truck up and towards the road. They tried again, this time breaking the chain completely.

I was secretly relieved. Not only was I genuinely afraid that I would remove my cowboy boots and find my toes rolling around in them, but it was getting dark; I had planned on being on the road by early afternoon, and I was afraid of the ever-increasing possibility that it would soon be two trucks in the ditch.

Two headlights pierced the night. The owners of the house were approaching.

My heart sank when three men emerged with shovels and I realized they were there to help.

Luckily, two of the men were about my age, and I felt vindicated as they quickly gave up against the cold and returned to their SUV. My pride diminished, I asked if I could join them in the warm car. I passed the time with them in the back seat of their SUV, listening to classic rock until Tom and Antonio came back to fetch me.

I rode back to the office with Johnny in the back next to me. We had failed to get the truck out, but I was grateful for the heat. The discussion was animated, regarding the rescue attempt as an adventure. But they reserved most of their compliments for someone named "L.B."

"L.B. is a total legend," Tom said over his shoulder to Johnny.

"Not even dressed properly. Would not quit."

"First time out."

Johnny looked over at me, seemingly appraising my feet. I clearly wasn't dressed properly either.

We returned to the office where Dani was waiting. Tom and Antonio embraced me briefly.

"Proud of you, Lady Boots. Come see us anytime."

And they walked away into the night. Only when I got in the

car back towards the safety of Tara's house did I realize who L.B., the legend, was. Lady Boots.

I left my lady boots at Tara's house and got on the road. The blizzard showed no signs of stopping for the next 48 hours, but I didn't want to derail my trip. Plus, I was feeling confident. I was Lady Boots, the undaunted, Lady Boots, the legend.

I drove all the way through the evening, stopping in Billings (population 117,116). I crashed in a hotel room with Dani's husband and son, who were there for a hockey tournament. I brought a twelve pack of Bud Light as an offering. Stressed from the day, I finished all twelve with Dani's husband.

I woke up the next morning and drove across the incredibly flat state of North Dakota. The snow clung to the craggy ridges of the badlands, my only respite from the flatness. I passed a billboard that simply said "Be Nice" and stopped in a gas station and saw a pot of "Beans and Weenies" on the counter; I felt like I was truly in North Dakota.

I stayed overnight in Fargo (population 121,889) with my friend Jason and his family. Jason took me out for a night downtown Fargo, where we hopped from cool bar to cool bar but endured absolutely horrid winds in between stops. North Dakota, I decided, was too cold for me to call my permanent home, but I was trying to stay open-minded.

While I was there, I got in touch with Tim Mahoney, the mayor of Fargo. We met in a Starbucks in a strip mall off the highway. Tim was a man who reminded me of my grandfather's friends when I was growing up in Wisconsin, with a trustworthy face, white hair, and a Midwestern twang that put me right at home.

"I think the big takeaway is this: I've gone to Washington D.C. and talked to other mayors," Mahoney said over the sound of the espresso machine. "If your city has something that people like about it, they'll stay. If you have an environment in which people can grow and find their dreams, I think that you have a good chance of success. And that's what we've started to have."

Tim told the story of a man he had interviewed for a position whose wife was adamant against moving to Fargo.

"What the heck is in Fargo?" he said, imitating her. When the man came for the interview, he brought his wife and by the end of the weekend, they had put in an offer on a house. All it took was them visiting and seeing for themselves. Tim leaned in and said I had been given an incredible gift: the ability to see the beauty in so many places across the country, places that people would always just have a preconceived notion of.

After Fargo, I drove to nearby Fergus Falls, a small town in Minnesota. As I entered Fergus Falls, I noticed a sign bearing the name of the town welcoming me in with the phrase "Real Nice Folks" inscribed below it. Fergus Falls had been at the center of a fake news scandal the year before, a scandal that grew large enough to be covered in the *New York Times* article, "Minnesota Town Defamed by German Reporter Is Ready to Forgive." After Trump's election, Fergus Falls (population 13,138) had hosted German reporter Claas Relotius, a journalist for *Der Spiegel*, a well-respected European publication. Instead of portraying the quaint, pleasant town I found myself driving into, Relotius portrayed the town "as a backward, racist place whose residents blindly supported President Trump. He made up details about a young city official. He concocted characters, roadside signs and racially tinged plotlines," while he could've instead written "about the many residents who maintain friendships across partisan lines, about the efforts to lure former residents back to west-central Minnesota or about how a city of roughly 14,000 people maintains a robust arts scene."

I arrived on a Sunday and met with Mayor Ben Schrierer at Union Pizza and Brewing Company, a restaurant he owned with his wife. I walked into the dark restaurant, a Union-army themed pizza parlor in the center of the downtown, covered in flags and Civil War paraphernalia. The glasses had quotes from Union heroes like Abraham Lincoln. Ben was a thin man with a furrowed brow and a sense of boundless energy.

"Sorry we're closed today," Ben said. "Otherwise I'd get you a pizza. I can pour you a beer, if you want…"

"I'm driving to Minneapolis, but thank you."

Ben gave me a tour of the pizza parlor with a palpable sense of pride, showing off historic Civil War-era posters, before sitting down at a back booth. I took out my recorder.

"I wanted to ask about the *Der Spiegel* story. I heard about that a few states back."

"Yeah, it was bizarre. Here comes this CNN Journalist of the Year to our community, and I think what a great opportunity, you know? Within the first 10 minutes that I'm talking to this guy at City Hall on a Monday morning, I realized. I can see in his expression and his reaction to the responses we gave to his questions that this is not what he expected at all. He expected to come in here and just be able to paint us as the stereotype, this rural, redneck hickville. He seemed so surprised. And I thought, personally, what a wonderful opportunity for this award-winning journalist to see a more nuanced picture of what rural America and rural communities are, which is not simple. It's not easy."

A car passed outside the parlor window. Ben turned his head and looked outside.

"So I was really excited for him to publish. He was in this community for three weeks. He sat here in this pizza shop and wrote in the afternoons. At first when I read the article, I thought Google Translate wasn't doing a good job. Then we started realizing it was totally fabricated. It was bizarre in some ways, like writing that me and another city administrator carry a Beretta rifle or there's a boar's head on my wall, but it was also offensive in some ways, like fabricating that there's a sign at the edge of the city that says, 'Mexicans Go Home.'"

"Instead of what it actually says." I said, thinking of the "Real Nice Folks" sign on the outskirts of town.

"Exactly! But then the second go round was actually *as* bizarre, if not more bizarre, because then the international media picks up on this story as a big deal because of fake news and because of the liberal media bias and all these things. So the next thing you know, I'm on *Fox News, Fox and Friends, New York Times, Der Spiegel, The Wall Street Journal* — they're all in Fergus, but in the end, it was just an opportunity for us to tell the real story, and I think we got more publicity and more attention out of that story than you could ever buy. And just when you think it is kind of over, a couple of weeks ago, I got a call from the Deputy Consulate General from Germany who wanted to come to Fergus."

He looked around at the dark pizza shop.

"You know, that's the thing about a place like this. I'll tell you what, when we opened this pizza place, this entire community was invested in our success. It just kind of blew my mind. These people, they're not just kind of wishing us good luck. They seriously would do anything for us to succeed. That's something I don't think you'd get in a lot of places at least that I've been to around the world. I mean, there are great people everywhere, but people here are so good at taking care of their own or being there when people need it."

I returned to Iowa, where I hadn't been since I worked on the Hillary Clinton campaign leading up to the Iowa Caucus back in 2016. I wound my way down from Minneapolis and drove through Des Moines (population 215,636). I stopped and watched two presidential candidates courting Iowans—first I watched Bernie Sanders give an impassioned stump speech on the campus of a local college, then I went to a brewery to hear from Gov. John Hickenlooper. It felt familiar, being in a rally, but I was glad to be bound by none of the former pressure of working as a staffer. I left Des Moines and headed back to Sioux City (population 82,531), the place I'd been stationed by the Clinton campaign leading up to Caucus Day in 2016.

I had left Los Angeles for a fellowship on the campaign in Iowa. I had felt a lack of fulfillment living in Los Angeles; I found that the things I cared about—the news of the day, ideas about policies and politics—caused eyes to glaze over at parties. When I was expressing my feelings of being out of place at drinks with a friend, he told me that his best friend from college was hiring organizers in Iowa and he'd be happy to pass my resume along. Within a day, I was on the phone with the campaign. And so, in August of 2015, I found myself packing up my apartment in Los Angeles and driving to Iowa as I got sucked into the orbit of the craziest presidential election in modern history. Training was held at the Iowa headquarters in Des Moines, and each of us gathered to be trained in the ways of the mystical Iowa caucus. The history and science behind the caucus genuinely surprised me: some thought it was an antiquated system that didn't make a lot of sense. However, we were told never to insult it in front of Iowans: they were proud to be the first in the nation state.

I was also given an outline of my duties. During the day, we would go door to door to see if people would commit to caucus for Hillary. At 5 o'clock p.m., we would call to ask the same question.

"How do we know for sure if they weren't just saying they would caucus for her, just so we go away?"

"Commit to caucus cards," explained my boss, munching on a burrito. "If they sign it, they will caucus for Hillary."

"How do you know?"

"Oh, the Iowans are mysterious creatures! Once they sign a commit to caucus card, they mate for life."

The responses while knocking doors should not have been surprising to me, but they were.

"The Caucus?"

"That's in February."

"It's only September."

"Leave me alone."

"Someone was here yesterday."

I found people to be generally exasperated, and when I mentioned that, my boss simply replied, "good. Wear them out."

"So who do we call now?"

"The same people."

"Okay, so what do we do if we get them on the phone?"

"Convince them to come volunteer."

"Okay, what do those people come to do?"

"Make calls to recruit people."

"To do what?"

"Make calls."

I had many misadventures during my time in Iowa. I once released a dog from a yard while knocking doors and had to chase it all over Sioux City. I taught Hillary Clinton to do the sorority squat. I learned to appreciate the local delicacy called "The Juicy Lucy." I was kicked out of a restaurant for trying to speak to Heidi Cruz. I felt adopted by the community and I loved every moment.

Reminiscing about the oddities of the presidential campaign in a small town, I drove through familiar corn fields and past familiar smokestacks. I was on my way to an even more rural region than Sioux City. I was going to be staying with Wes, one of the friends I had made during the campaign, in his hometown close to Sioux Center (population 8,273), near the South Dakota border on the Iowa side, one of the most conservative parts of Iowa. In fact, it was so conservative that there was only one family who voted in the Democratic caucus in the town, making their vote extremely powerful.

Wes had multiple friends over to his house when I stayed with him. Each of them was extremely conservative, loved cigarettes, drank about ten beers, then told me we were going across the border into South Dakota, where most of them lived. They got me absolutely trashed before pulling me into the back of their pickups and driving me God knows where.

We pulled into a small downtown, got out of the car, and walked up to the only lit windows on the street—a cozy dive bar. It was a Saturday night, yet we were the only ones in the place. As we drank picklebacks, every single person in our group talked about cheating on their significant other at some point in the conversation. The bartender, who was an immigrant from Eastern Europe, talked about how much she loved Vladimir Putin.

These were my only memories of South Dakota.

I woke up the next day to a text from my dad. "Is there any way you could cut your trip a day short?" I asked him why.

"Cindy's not doing well, and she's moved her end-of-life celebration to this weekend instead of next week. She wants to meet you."

Cindy was a friend of my dad's who had been battling with cancer over the past few months, but whose condition had worsened rapidly in the past few days. Her family had planned an "end of life party" or an opportunity for all of her friends and family to say goodbye. I had never met Cindy, but I know she meant a great deal to Dad. I thought about my itinerary in Nebraska (Omaha, Lincoln), Kansas (Manhattan, Topeka, Lawrence) and Missouri (Kansas City, Hannibal, and St. Louis). I knew I would have to rush, but I could make it. I was getting tired. I just wanted to go home.

I drove to Omaha, Nebraska (population 475,862) where I was meeting with a DACA recipient and field director for a congressional candidate. I met Maria through a friend from campaign work. Maria was someone who instantly made you feel at home. When she heard it was my first time in Omaha, she immediately drove me to the Omaha Zoo, one of the greatest zoos in America. As we walked around between the reptile house and gorilla house, Maria told me about her experience crossing the border into the United States.

"So I was born in Mexico City. I don't remember a lot of it, unfortunately. We immigrated when I was six. I don't know if it was because of the trauma of the journey. A coyote smuggled into the U.S."

"Coyote?"

"You've never heard that word before? It's someone who smuggles people across the border."

"So a coyote took you and your parents?"

Maria shook her head. "My parents came to the U.S. to work and support me."

"You weren't with your parents?" I asked, horrified.

"Nope. I was with my cousin and my little sister who was four at the time."

We walked into the zoo's giant biosphere, which was akin to walking into Willy Wonka's chocolate room: it was a self-contained jungle in the middle of Nebraska.

"So your parents coordinated with them from Mexico City and they were in Omaha?"

"They were recommended. You wanted to go with people who knew what they were doing and wouldn't sell you out."

"So it was pretty high stakes."

"My parents had been living here for about a year, saving up to bring us over. It was very tiring. I remember getting here. I remember getting dropped off. And I didn't recognize my parents. Because for a year I hadn't seen them. It took us about a month to go from Mexico to Omaha. Because the coyote would drop people off. We dropped people off through the Southwest and up to Washington state. And my parents didn't know where we were. The only way they knew was my cousin would call from a payphone and say, 'we're in Nevada today. We're closer to home.'"

"And was it the type of thing where once you were over the border it was more chill, you could be out and about?"

"For the most part, but there was still a concern. What I actually remember was not knowing what's going to happen but needing to be strong for my little sister. I didn't want her to freak out. She was only four."

We walked across a rickety wood bridge above the man-made river below.

"Prior to all this, it wasn't supposed to be that dramatic. We were supposed to go on a plane and land in Omaha once we crossed the border with a little backpack or whatever. But my uncle got in a fight with the coyote, and so he said 'your nieces are crossing like everyone else.' Problem is, my uncle is a very volatile man. My parents didn't know about it until we were in the middle of it. People would be like 'why would your parents do that to you?' and honestly they didn't know anything about it."

"We didn't know what we were in, until it happened. And we were in the middle of it. But when I saw them, heard their voices… reconnecting with my parents was so incredible. So now, when I hear about kids being apprehended at the border… separated from their families. It's something I understand. It's something known to me. We could've been caught. How can I not care? How can I not do something on this side?"

Maria and I spent the afternoon walking around the zoo. I really came to admire her mission to make Omaha a place that immigrants can feel comfortable in a conservative state. For her, politics wasn't a luxury. It was a necessity.

From Omaha, I drove quickly into Lincoln to see the capitol building. Nebraska has the only unicameral legislature in the country, and the giant Art Deco skyscraper of a capitol loomed large over the cornfields of Nebraska. Feeling rushed, I took the elevator to the observation deck, took a good look at the flat Nebraska landscape, then drove south to Kansas.

I had three more states to go: Kansas, Missouri, and Illinois. I wasn't sure where I was going to live, and driving through the flat prairie land, I felt a sense of sadness that the trip was ending without much of the catharsis I was hoping for. I stopped in a gas station off a one lane road and bought a bag of Skittles for a quick sugar high.

I tried to think of what was in Kansas. As I looked out over the Flint Hills while driving through Manhattan, Kansas (population 55,290), I considered if I should track down the members of the Westboro Baptist Church just for one final jaunt out of my comfort zone. I texted Brett, who advised me against it.

"You don't want another Trump rally incident, do you?"

I ended the night in a hotel in Topeka (population 125,963). The hotel was on the outskirts of town on a highway, the kind of place where lower-tier businessmen sat in the bar. A depressing place.

From my hotel room, I was craving human companionship, especially after I had been constantly stimulated with company for weeks. I decided to drive into town, where I stopped at a Mexican restaurant and ate delicious chips and, to hell with it, ordered a margarita. Everyone around me seemed to be laughing. I looked around at a family celebrating a birthday, a group of college kids arguing good-naturedly about some movie they'd seen. In the booth next to me, a couple was on a first date. The waiter arrived and asked if I was waiting for someone. I said no, and he cleared the napkins and brought me another margarita.

I got on Tinder, hoping for someone to distract me from my boredom and solitude. I found a blond Kansan boy with blue eyes and a kind face and began asking questions about the state to someone who could explain it to me.

"Tell me about Kansas."

"Kansas is great. I just can't believe you're in Topeka."

"Where are you?"

"About forty minutes away in Olathe. Outside of Kansas City."

"What is there here, besides tornadoes and Dorothy?"

"Surprisingly more than you think."

We both discussed our mutual love for *The Wizard of Oz*. I discovered that we both had dressed as the Wicked Witch of the West for Halloween when we were young. When he confirmed with a photo, I was utterly charmed. I began trying to convince him to meet me somewhere, *anywhere* to show me something, anything.

"Sorry, I would never drive to Topeka."

Thinking of the sad businesspeople in the bar, I made up a desperate lie, "but I'm moving to Kansas City in a few months!"

"Cool! Maybe I'll catch you then."

Shit. 48 states in; I had convinced mayors and governors to meet with me, but this one random Kansas dude was turning me down cold. I realized there was no way I was convincing this stubborn Kansan to come save me from my solitude.

I conceded and sent a message: "I guess I'll catch you next time I'm in town." Never.

I closed out my check and left the Mexican restaurant.

Back in my hotel room, I put my phone down on the nightstand. Outside, I could hear the rain pattering on the franchise hotel roof and the cars gliding on the slick highway. Forty-eight states, and I wasn't sure I was any closer to an answer about American democracy. I laid down in the starchy hotel sheets. The room smelled of stale cigarette smoke. My thoughts kept spinning in my head even as I tried to shut them down, like a washing machine that's just had the power cut. Perhaps, despite all of my optimism, I would not be able to find what I was looking for. My face on the pillow, I exhaled. Alone in Kansas, it was hard to feel hopeful.

I looked at my phone on the bedside table. There was one missed notification from Kansas Dude: "See you next time in Kansas City."

GOING HOME

I woke up with a start in my hotel room in Topeka. It was hard to believe with only two more states to go, the trip was nearly at its end. Lying and listening to the morning traffic rumble on the highway outside the hotel, I found myself overwhelmed by the swirling memories of people and places I had encountered and the stories I accrued across the country. I got out of bed and rubbed my eyes. Selfishly, I thought it would have added up to something clear about what I could do to lead a better life, but as I showered that morning, I felt more befuddled than ever. In my 48th state, I was no closer to finding a place to call home than I was to a job to help me pay off my soaring credit card bills. And still, the question of American democracy hung in the steamy hotel bathroom around me. After all this time, I had few answers. I mostly had stories.

I packed up my suitcase for what I hoped would be one of the last times in a long while, chucked it into a bug-spattered Belinda, and drove towards Kansas City. I was halfway out of Topeka when I made a split-second decision. I had decided against trying to track down the Westboro Baptist folks, but that didn't mean I couldn't drive by and see its Kansas headquarters. I turned around and drove back into the capital city. I drove through neighborhoods with newly budding trees, towards a quiet side street where Google Maps told me the church was located. I was surprised; in my mind I had always pictured one of the large, windowless megachurches built on farmland I was used to seeing in Rockford, not a half-acre property in a sleepy residential area. I approached the destination to find less of a church and more of a fortress. It was a Tudor-style house that had been supplemented with a large fence, and the only signifier that this was a place of worship was a small sign reading "WESTBORO BAPTIST CHUCH" in small font, giving "FAG MARRIAGE DOOMS NATIONS" the spotlight. On the side of the house, a banner was hung with Westboro's most infamous proclamation: "GOD HATES FAGS."

It was completely closed off with no entrance, a covetous place. It seemed set apart, afraid of the world, lashing out through posters and signs, keeping life outside their walls at bay. I thought it would be bigger, but the hate it espoused made it seem more daunting than it was.

I looked across the street to find a complete contrast. A modest ranch house had been painted with brilliant rainbow stripes, standing in solidarity next to a second house, painted light blue, pink, and white—the colors of the transgender pride flag. The dark property and the bright homes stood in a standoff across the street, daring the other to do something about the fact that they would be occupying the same corner for the foreseeable future, like it or not.

I decided to leave Topeka. I'm not sure if I was heartened by what I had seen, but gestures like painting a house across from a hate group made me slightly more optimistic about the state of Kansas. Perhaps it would take the excitable visitors gathering at the rainbow houses—from all walks of life, from all over the nation—to serve as a reminder of the loneliness that comes from isolating yourself from your fellow man. De Tocqueville recognized the soul's craving for "the infinite" but not at the expense of our associations with our neighbors. "The soul has needs that must be satisfied and whatever care one takes to distract it from itself, it soon becomes bored, restive, and agitated," he wrote during his travels. Between the two, Westboro seemed to be the more agitated side of the street.

Belinda and I got back on the highway and drove towards Kansas City, Missouri (population 491,158). It was not a place I had ever really thought much about. I knew that there was one in Kansas and one in Missouri, and the couple that was hosting me (the daughter of a Rockford theatre director and her husband) lived in the suburbs rather than the city. I can't say I was excited to spend my visit to Kansas City out in the 'burbs, but maybe that was America's appropriate sendoff. My final night of the trip was spent in suburban sprawl out of an Arcade Fire album, dead shopping malls and all.

I drove away from Kansas, empty of answers. I passed through Kansas City, Kansas, sure I had seen the last of the state, and I arrived in North Kansas City, Missouri to find a charming cul-de-sac waiting. The neighborhood kids were playing in Marissa and Mike's yard, pushing their two-year-old daughter Leica on a small tricycle. Pulling up, Marissa quickly came out to greet me and introduced me to her neighbor who was sitting inside chatting with her. Her neighbor was a social worker, and we got talking about how Kansas City had changed over the past few years. "It's grown like crazy," she told me. "It's one of the best-kept secrets in America." She suddenly looked worried. "So... shhhh!"

That night, Marissa and Mike drove me into the city to eat at Q39, a Kansas City barbecue joint. We ate ribs and burnt ends and discussed their decision to move to Kansas City, despite having a rival job opportunity in Manhattan, NYC. They cited the low cost of living, friendly Midwestern vibe, and thriving arts scene in Kansas City as the surprising combination that made them forgo the Big Apple for the Paris of the Plains. After wiping our hands free of sauce, they offered to give me a driving tour of Kansas City.

"Will Leica be okay?" I asked as Mike hoisted up their two-year-old daughter from her highchair.

"She sleeps great in the car. We'll drive for as long as she's asleep."

We ended up driving around for three straight hours. I learned that Kansas City was nicknamed "The City of Fountains" as they drove me between neighborhoods and pointed to countless public squares with large fountains.

"There are nearly 200 in the city," Marissa told me. "Second only to Rome."

First, they drove to show me the Plaza District, a shopping area decorated in a Spanish style, then to a well-lit downtown with Art Deco skyscrapers, which I learned was called the Power and Light District, and then to the River Market, a beautiful outdoor market right on the Missouri River. Leica was still sleeping, so we kept driving to the surrounding towns of Weston, Liberty, and North Kansas City, right along the Kansas border. They touched on the complicated history between Kansas and Missouri dating back to the Civil War, with Missouri, a slave state, grappling with Kansas self-determining whether it would be admitted to the Union as a free or slave state, resulting in a war between the states known as Bleeding Kansas.

They finished off the tour by bringing me to one of the city's most scenic locations: the World War One Memorial, a towering monument overlooking the entire downtown. As we walked up the promenade to the memorial, I saw people walking by lamplight, even though it was past 10 p.m. We climbed the marble stairs of the monument towards an overlook, where tourists and "I HEART KC" sweater-wearers alike were admiring the views of the skyline. As I approached, my breath was taken away by the epic cityscape. The Kansas City monuments were intentionally lit up with multi-colored lights: Union Station was a brilliant blue, the Power and Light skyscraper was crimson, as other skyscrapers danced with rainbow light shows.

It was spectacular.

Looking out over the illuminated skyline, I felt a feeling I hadn't felt in years. I cannot say precisely what happened. I cannot say whether it was the people or the buildings, the scenery or the rainbow lights. But I suddenly experienced the feeling I had wanted, the feeling I had craved since I first set off on my journey. I felt the inexplicable feeling of home: it felt like driving in the car with Michael, being backstage at New American Theatre, singing along to the radio in the car with my brother on the way to school. Something about this cinematic scene was growing into something more significant than just a pretty city all lit up, almost like an instinct: this is where you belong. I was aware of the fact that I was chronicling a book, and would be vulnerable to making grand gestures, but the moment I had been hoping for, the all-consuming gut instinct, was hitting me hard here in Kansas City.

"Is there anything wrong with this place?"

Marissa looked out and shook her head, then stopped herself. "Of course it's not perfect. But it's perfect for us."

Walking away from the monument, I texted Scotty, one of my best friends from high school. He had told me over Christmas that he was going to be moving to Missouri with his girlfriend, but I couldn't remember where. "Where did you say you were moving again?"

Almost immediately, a text bubble began typing.

"Kansas City... haha why?"

"I might move there," I said.

As he responded to this completely wild thought, I looked back over the city. It wasn't logical, but I had that feeling of belonging, that first date flutter, and after five months of waiting for that feeling, I felt this ought to count for something.

In bed that night, I considered how much scarier moving to a city without family or educational connections was than moving to a metropolis where I knew people, but I didn't feel any of that in the morning. Getting out of bed, I just felt a strange resolve that this would not be the last I would see of Kansas City. I said goodbye to Mike and Marissa, got in the car, and made my way home towards Rockford.

After months of using my recorder to capture the thoughts of people across the country, I turned it on and put it in the passenger seat and let myself say all of the things that had been on my mind. The complexity of the political moment. My own misgivings about if this trip achieved anything of value in divisive times. My search for meaning after a tumultuous season of my life. And the fledgling belief that, even though it made no sense, I had found something that felt almost like home.

"Kansas City... I'll be back." My voice said, captured on the recorder to this day. "Yeah. I'll definitely be back."

By early afternoon, I pulled into my parents' house in Rockford and began to assess the state of Belinda's back seat. The cowboy hat was sitting next to Julia's forgotten thermos, which was next to Brett's forsaken water bottle, rolling around on the floor by a Hickenlooper for President beer koozie. Mr. Crack was in the window. Belinda displayed a proud 23,237 miles on her odometer. It was over.

I went into the house and was immediately greeted by Emma, a Goldendoodle, who peed all over the garage, the driveway, and my shoes. Charlotte, a Pit Bull mix, followed after, holding a boot in her mouth. My parents came out and hugged me, telling me that we had to get a move on if we were going to make it to Cindy's on time. It didn't seem real; my equilibrium was going haywire. I couldn't believe I was finally home.

The next thing I knew, I was in the car headed to Cindy's celebration of life party. We arrived at a house overlooking cornfields, with a line of hundreds of people snaking out the front door and to the driveway. I stood in line and watched as people greeted each other.

"How do you know Cindy?"

"From Church, and you?"

"She was my old neighbor."

I stood with my dad who was unusually stoic. Uneasy with silence, I struck up a conversation with the girl behind me, who I quickly realized was the daughter of my elementary school nurse. This was a small town indeed. As I talked about the trip, people started to join in the conversation. The pastor from my old church, a coworker of my dad. The line between my family and Cindy got shorter and shorter, as I was asked something I hadn't considered.

"Do you feel more or less hopeful now that you're done?"

I didn't have to think. "More. Definitely more hopeful."

Cindy was sitting in the kitchen in front of windows over-looking cornfields and new developments. She was surrounded by yellow balloons and flowers that gave the constant reminder that this was meant to be a celebration. I watched people approach, hug Cindy, say their goodbyes, pose for a picture, and then move on to greet the others at the party. Everyone was doing their best to keep the energy positive, but there was a quiet sort of Midwestern catharsis underlying the event.

Finally, it was our turn to approach. My dad kissed Cindy on the cheek. She ushered him closer, and whispered loudly enough for us all to hear:

"I just lost a tooth."

"We didn't notice," my dad said, smiling.

Cindy turned to me. I clutched her hand, as her brilliant, multi-colored eyes looked into mine.

"You have the most beautiful eyes," was all I could bring myself to say.

"I'm so glad to meet you," she said softly, smiling at my dad.

"My dad says that you are the most incredible person. He's lucky to have you in his life."

She shook her head. "I'm the lucky one."

They shared a moment, as my mom and I stepped back, and my dad leaned his head in towards Cindy's face and whispered something I couldn't hear.

Cindy shook her head. "It's time," she said, "it's time."

"I'll think about you every day," my dad said to her.

I was horrified to feel my eyes filling with unbidden, unwelcome tears. I looked around the party and saw all the people that this woman had touched, and how we too had been pulled into the orbit of her life. This was the beauty of a community. As my father leaned down and whispered his last goodbye to Cindy, the overwhelming realization came that Cindy would someday be everyone I love. Someday someone would be the one telling my mother goodbye, my father goodbye, my brother goodbye, and everyone else I had loved on my life's journey. And someday, if I lived a life like Cindy's, others would be saying goodbye to me as well.

"Photo?"

I turned around, hoping I had misheard. FLASH. A photographer captured a picture of the four of us at that moment. When I saw it later, it was clear that I was the only one crying.

I gave Cindy's hand one final squeeze, and we were guided away from the chair towards the kitchen, where one of Cindy's daughters approached my father. She too was wearing yellow. "We don't know how to thank you for all you've done for her," she said. Her eyes were welling with tears.

My dad looked down at his feet. "She's done more for me than you will ever know."

We were ushered downstairs for food and drinks. I stepped into the bathroom to collect myself, thinking how inappropriate this moment was to be hit by the emotion of a journey's end. But still, I was suddenly overcome with people and places: Gambier, Cleveland, Shepherdstown, Appleton, Casper, Anchorage, Kansas City. Michael, Sarah, Brett, Julia, Mom, Dad, Denise, Aunt Kim, Tony, Kachen, DeeDee, Pastor Lori, Carl, Cindy. These people, this life.

The struggle, the brevity. The diversity, the finality. The pain, the triumph. How lucky we are to have this journey.

All around the country, people were brimming with stories of the successes of their towns, but also of their losses and pain. If we were ever going to be able to heal democracy, we would have to start with hearing those stories and sharing our common humanity. Everyone across the country had struggles, but many people didn't have a place to turn. They didn't always have someone to listen. And I thought of how fortunate I was that I had been able to hear stories that might have been left untold. Amidst all the division, none of us had all the answers. All we had was each other.

I cleaned up my eyes and returned to my mom and dad, who were talking to one of Cindy's grandsons. I was looking at them with the kind of love you can only feel when you understand the ephemeral gift of parents.

I watched as Cindy's grandson, a tall blond teenager in a striped shirt, removed a deck of cards from my dad's pocket.

"He's a magician!" my mom said.

"Are you really?" I said, relieved to have some levity.

The grandson nodded, and dealt five cards into my hand, and had me put them into my pocket. When he had me remove them, there were nearly 50.

I was astounded. "That's… amazing!"

"I'm hoping to go big time. Do birthday parties, weddings, things like that."

"Everybody needs a bit of magic sometimes," my mom said.

We thanked him and watched as he approached another family, asking them to extend their palm. As he dealt the cards into the hands of the daughter of my school nurse, I watched as the community gathered around to watch. As he removed a thick stack of cards from her jacket pocket, her eyes widened in delight, and she burst into applause. I watched him as he made his way around the party, mesmerizing my old neighbors, the pastor of my old church, and Cindy's daughters, dealing cards and smiling placidly as they discovered that their hands had transformed into something unexpected and new.

As we said goodbye, the line hadn't dwindled. I stood at the door and took one last look at Cindy. She was being hugged by two young children, but as I stepped out the door, I saw her look up to see my dad in the doorframe. She gave him a small wave. He smiled back, then waved goodbye.

As we walked out into the Illinois breeze, I let my dad walk ahead of me for a moment. I watched the faces of my hometown waiting to celebrate Cindy, her spark, and the magic that was her life in this community. As I felt the wind pick up, I caught up to my parents and took them each by the arm. I savored the moment, feeling my soul swell with the overwhelming awareness of being alive, being a part of a community. 50 states later and I found myself more at home than ever in my native Midwest, more grateful than ever for the upbringing it had given me. As I got into Belinda for a final drive home, I considered the miracle that we were all here together, existing in this era, doing our best with the time we've been given in this beautiful shared American experience.

EPILOGUE

THE NELSON-ATKINS MUSEUM of Art sits at the top of a hill in the heart of Kansas City. Inside, the free museum houses paintings by Caravaggio, Monet, Van Gogh. The Rozzelle Court Café is a large indoor Italian-style courtyard centered around a fountain surrounded by bronze engravings of each of the zodiacs. It is my favorite place in Kansas City, and where I decided to finish writing this book.

I moved to Kansas City in August of 2019, approximately five months after the end of my trip through the United States. I returned to Oxford to finish classes and collect my thoughts, and I found my mind inexplicably returning to that technicolor skyline and surprising feeling of home I felt in the city on the border of Kansas and Missouri. My Oxford classmates and tutors alike seemed flummoxed by this random fixation ("Where was it you want to move? Arkansas?") , but Kansas City kept coming up in my mind. There was only one problem: I didn't know anyone except for Marissa and Michael and the random Kansas Tinder Guy. I kept returning to the idea, until my friend Scotty called to let me know that he, fortuitously, solidified plans to move to Kansas

City that summer. I spent my final weeks of school in June Face-Timing into apartment tours from Christ Church Meadow and started to make plans. Classmates were quick to point out the obvious: I had no job, no plan, and was essentially committing to living in a town I had visited for 24 hours. But there was an excitement about the lack of logic. And so when I returned back to America that August, I packed up Belinda with my belongings from my childhood room and drove into the unknown. I'm a gut-decision maker, and from the moment I saw the Art Deco grandeur of the Power and Light building all lit up and saw a community filled with people wearing t-shirts imprinted with declarations of love for their city, I had to follow to see what she had in store for me.

My first night in Kansas City, I was all alone in my new apartment when Tinder Guy from Kansas reached out, asking if I had plans. I didn't; I had no friends and Scotty hadn't arrived yet, so I was roommate-less. I arrived at Tom's Town Distillery and saw the blond man sitting in the corner wearing a Chicago Cubs henley ("not gonna happen," I thought, sure that I wouldn't want to settle down with the first person to show interest in me in a new city). One drink turned into two, and we walked down Main Street to the Green Lady Lounge, listened to a jazz trio, and talked with unexpected candor about all of our failed attempts at love. We cabbed back to my apartment (devoid of furniture besides a couch), listened to Fleetwood Mac, and fell asleep on the cramped sofa. We woke up the next day and went for a walk by the river and have been dating ever since. Go figure.

Like any leap of faith, such as driving to all 50 states with no plan, moving to a new city is pretty scary. Forgoing the safety net that comes with educational and hometown connections make scrappiness a necessity. I was at square one again trying to find a job in a new city. When I yearned for my familiar surroundings in New York, I inevitably met new people who re-inspired the notion that I was in the right place. I had learned on my trip to show up and hope luck would strike, and sure enough, like on my journey around the country, chance encounters led to jobs, new friends, new opportunities. The more time I spent in this city, the more I felt I was given a fresh start. Old versions of myself, old notions of what I was supposed to be doing disappeared. After a painful initial transition (and the arrival of a global pandemic) I began to find things I was passionate about in the community. Being a Big Brother for Big Brothers Big Sisters and serving on their board. Learning neighborhood leadership through the University of Missouri-Kansas City. Being a part of the first regional production of *The Inheritance* at a local equity theatre that gave me the same feeling of home I felt at New American Theatre in Rockford. Working with the American Public Square, a Kansas City-based community organization working to improve the tone and quality of public discourse. Slowly but surely, I started to feel as though I was a part of a community—the small town feeling of being known and loved that Joanna spoke of. And that, united by our love for where we lived, helped me connect to those in my community. While Kansas City is incredibly progressive, the surrounding area is ruby red. Being here has reminded me that I didn't just go around the country to get the pulse of America. I tried to suss out the best things we can do for democracy with our limited time, how we can take action instead of screaming into the void. This little move, this jump into the dark is my hope that perhaps with a new mindset, we can set the country on the right course again. We can be a cohesive whole and allow our better angels to win out in a community where we can actually make an impact. Our communities are microcosms of democracy; to build a better nation, perhaps we should start where we live and give ourselves permission to see the good happening around us.

Still, I see warning signs on the horizon. Our country is at a crossroads. It has become evident in many ways that we are still experiencing the effects of a decade during which many of our democratic institutions came into question. Our civic fabric has been torn. Families and friendships have been cleaved apart by the media, social media, and cynical politicians who profit off our divisions. The effects of social media on our dialogue are getting more dire by the day, as it changes the way our brains perceive nuance and the humanity of other people. I have tried to find ways to focus on the issues I can affect locally, the people whose opinions I can engage. We can't, after all, expect other people to think exactly like us. Our upbringings and experiences are too varied. We cannot approach difficult conversations with the intention of making people think exactly like us. Rather than aiming to change minds, we can try to broaden them, push them to consider other experiences, pull them into the orbit of other lives and stories. That's where meaningful change happens.

Now, working at an organization called The Trevor Project, I run an editorial program focused on telling stories to help de-stigmatize conversations around mental health and fight to end suicide among LGBTQ+ young people. As I traveled, I learned that our own stories are inextricably linked to how we view our democracy, and I'm glad to be able to give back in a small way using the power of storytelling, working for an organization that advocates for a kinder, more understanding world. After eating my way through America, I now also write restaurant reviews for Kansas City, one of the rising food stars in the Midwest.

I bought a house in Kansas City a year ago. I now have a backyard, a small brown dog, and great company in Random Kansas Dude. He is superstitious; the Kansas City Chiefs won the Super Bowl the year I arrived. I am now required to be in town on Super Bowl Sunday forevermore, just in case. That's fine with me. I am always thankful to be in Kansas City and intend to stay for a long time.

One of my first nights in Kansas City, a friend of mine who had been in the city to do a play at Kansas City Repertory Theatre connected me to Maggie, one of the leaders of the cohesive, vibrant theatre community. Maggie hosted a reading of a new play script monthly in her home, a space for actors in the community to gather and talk about the issues that the plays explore.

I went to a "Script Circle" gathering on the second weekend in town. We read a play about cultural dilemmas facing our country. We finished the play and began the discussion. "What do we feel is the best way to have difficult conversations?"

"Any ideas?" said the host, opening it up to the group.

I smiled at how fitting the moment was. Across the country, I found that discussing Politics with a capital "P" was much less compelling than the stories that shaped the worldviews of the people I met. At the end of the day, stories are the most important tool we have to increase empathy and broaden people's minds. I had some ideas, but I was much more interested in watching the hands jump up, waiting to tell their own stories.

50 states later and staying in one place suddenly seemed to be the biggest adventure.

ACKNOWLEDGMENTS

There are two types of people who make great things happen. There are those that cheer you on when you come up with a wild idea like traveling to all 50 states, despite it not being logical. Then there are those who cheer you up after you've done the thing and it hasn't panned out quite like you expected, those who tell you not to give up. This book is very much thanks to both of those types of people.

I'd like to thank the team at Bite-Sized Books, Julian and Paul. This book took nearly four years to get published. I heard many things about the book in those four years—it was too bipartisan, it was too analytical, it was too personal, it was too of the moment, or the moment had passed. I want to thank Julian and Paul for letting me tell the story the way I felt it should be told and supporting me in that effort. This version of the journey is the purest, most truthful one, and I'm grateful to be able to share it this way.

I also want to thank all of the people who took the time to let me stay in their homes, bought me meals, shared intimate pieces of their lives with me. I especially want to thank all of those who don't see their story reflected in these pages—some experiences are too good to put into words.

I want to thank all of the people who read drafts and gave me their candid feedback. To my Oxford tutors Peter Moore, Anna Beer, and Rebecca Abrams: thank you for turning this from a lark into a real story with direction and making me ask the hard questions. I want to especially thank Ioan for the brutal feedback—it made this book a million times better. I want to thank Ashton for reading and the loving discussion about the morality of listening in the light of political upheaval. I want to thank Bridget for swapping drafts. To Fergus for your candid feedback and great advice. To Stevie for remembering that I still had an unpublished book waiting to get out there. For all of my Oxford classmates—Maria, Lainey, Em, Nancy, Esame—who read this book in different iterations and gave me direction. And most of all, for Random Kansas Dude (aka Chad) for incisive feedback that always finds my blind spots. The fact that I caught you, usually hard to break, reading the end with tears in your eyes helped me know that it was ready to go.

I'd like to thank my family for the love and support always. Thank you for teaching me the importance of roots and wings; I'm glad I finally got some roots.

Thank you to the Kansas City community for welcoming me. I hope I've started to do my part to be a productive member of the ecosystem of my favorite city in the country. Thank you for letting me be a KCMO cheerleader.

Lastly, I hope this book will inspire others to get to know our beautiful country. The only thing I know for sure is to take a journey is to undergo a change. As Joseph Campbell says, "in order to find something new, one has to leave the old and go in quest of the seed idea, a germinal idea that will have the potentiality of bringing forth that new thing." To anyone who doubts the power of travel as transformative, I hope this book inspires you to take a journey for answers. I certainly would not be living the life I am now had I not taken a leap of faith four years ago.

DISCUSSION QUESTIONS

1. How has your upbringing affected your worldview as an American? As it relates to politics?

2. Was there something or someone that changed your mind about something while you were growing up? Who or what was it?

3. Think of a place you've always wanted to visit in the United States, a place you'd never want to visit, and your favorite place to visit. What do these places have in common?

4. What's your favorite big city in America? What's your favorite medium-sized city? What's your favorite small town? Did any of the towns in the book make you want to visit?

5. Do you think social media or the news media is dividing us more? Why?

6. Is there someone from a different political persuasion who has changed the way you think about something? Has someone having

different political views strained a relationship that is important to you?

7. Do you think America is divided? If so, what would it take for us to come together again?

8. What makes you hopeful about America today?

9. Talk about the last argument you had about politics. Was there something said that helped you have a constructive dialogue? Was there something that inflamed tensions?

10. How does travel affect the way we see people who are different from us? Tell a story about a travel experience that changed you.

11. In one sentence, what does it mean to be American?

12. What is the thing that makes you proudest about being an American? What is the thing that makes you least proud?

13. What is an issue you will never be able to see the other side on? What is an issue you are open-minded to?

14. What is making America so polarized today?

15. Talk about a time someone changed your mind. How did they go about it? How did they make you feel? Was there something they said that you remember?

16. What is the best U.S. state? What state surprised you the most in this book?

NOTES

Albright, Madeline *Fascism: A Warning*. William Collins, 2019.

"#3 Rockford, Ill." Forbes. Forbes Magazine. Accessed September 8, 2019. https://www.forbes.com/pictures/mli45lmhg/3-rockford-ill/#3ca600184fb3.

Bureau, US Census. "Geography Program." *Census.gov*, 7 Sept. 2022, https://www.census.gov/geography.

Braun, Georgette. "Rockford Again Makes 'Worst Cities' List." Rockford Register Star. Rockford Register Star, June 14, 2018. https://www.rrstar.com/news/20180613/rockford-again- makes-worst-cities-list.

Dougherty, Danny, Brian McGill, and Dante Chinni and Aaron Zitner. "Where Graduates Move After College - Northwestern." The Wall Street Journal. Dow Jones & Company, May 15, 2018. https://www.wsj.com/graphics/where-graduates-move-after-college/.

Dougherty, Danny, Brian McGill, and Dante Chinni and Aaron Zitner. "Where Graduates Move After College." The Wall Street Journal. Dow Jones & Company, May 15, 2018. https:// www.wsj.com/graphics/where-graduates-move-after-college/.

Fallows, James. "Erie and America." The Atlantic. Atlantic Media Company, August 26, 2016. https://www.theatlantic.com/national/archive/2016/08/erie-and-america/497060/.

Flowers, Kevin. "Final Erie County Vote Totals Shed Light on Trump's Win." GoErie.com. GoErie.com, November 20, 2016. https://www.goerie.com/news/20161120/final-erie- county-vote-totals-shed-light-on-trumps-win.

"Harrison Center." Harrison Center. Accessed September 15, 2019. https://www.harrisoncenter.org/.

"Hospitality Center - A Ministry of the Episcopal Diocese of Milwaukee - Home." Hospitality Center - A Ministry of the Episcopal Diocese of Milwaukee - Home. Accessed September 15, 2019. http://www.hospitality-center.org/.

"How Trump Won the Presidency with Razor-Thin Margins in Swing States." The Washington Post. WP Company. Accessed September 15, 2019. https://www.washingtonpost.com/ graphics/politics/2016-election/swing-state-margins/.

"Local Area Unemployment Statistics - Rockford, IL." U.S. Bureau of Labor Statistics. U.S. Bureau of Labor Statistics. Accessed September 6, 2019. https://data. bls.gov/timeseries/ LAUMT174042000000004? amp%253bdata_tool=XGtable&output_view=data&include_graphs=true.

"Number of College Graduates Per Year (2019)." EducationData. Accessed September 15, 2019. https://educationdata.org/number-of-college-graduates/.

"Ohio Election Results 2016: President Live Map by County, Real-Time Voting Updates." Election Hub. Accessed September 2019. https://www.politico.com/ 2016-election/ results/map/president/ohio/.

"Portland-South Portland-Biddeford, ME Economy at a Glance." U.S. Bureau of Labor Statistics. U.S. Bureau of Labor Statistics. Accessed September 17, 2019. https:// www.bls.gov/eag/eag.me_portland_mn.htm.

Taylor, Jessica. "Bernie Sanders Wins West Virginia Primary." NPR. NPR, May 11, 2016. https:// www.npr.org/2016/05/10/477553418/bernie-sanders-wins-west-virginia-primary.

Thompson, Derek. "American Migration Patterns Should Terrify the GOP." The Atlantic. Atlantic Media Company, September 17, 2019. https://www.theatlantic. com/ideas/ archive/2019/09/american-migration-patterns-should-terrify-gop/.

Tocqueville, Alexis de. *Democracy in America*. New York: Random House, 2004.

Trubek, Anne. "Rust Belt Stereotypes Are Misleading and Dangerous." Time. Time. Accessed

September 15, 2019. https://time.com/5225497/rust-belt-history/.

"Union Miles Park." Trulia. Accessed September 15, 2019. https://www.trulia. com/n/oh/ cleveland/union-miles-park/85596/.

US Census Bureau. "Population and Housing Unit Estimates Tables." Tables, June 18, 2019. https://www.census.gov/programs-surveys/popest/data/tables. 2018.html.

Woodard, Colin. *American Nations: A History of the Eleven Rival Regional Cultures of North America*. Penguin Books, 2012.

www.ingramcontent.com/pod-product-compliance
Lightning Source LLC
Chambersburg PA
CBHW022220010125
19782CB00015B/31/J